VENICE

ENCOUNTER

ALISON BING

Farley 2014

Venice Encounter
2nd edition – November 2010

Published by Lonely Planet Publications Pty Ltd
ABN 36 005 607 983

Australia	Head Office, Locked Bag 1
	Footscray, Vic 3011
	☎ 03 8379 8000 fax 03 8379 8111
	talk2us@lonelyplanet.com.au
USA	150 Linden St, Oakland, CA 94607
	☎ 510 250 6400
	toll free 800 275 8555
	fax 510 893 8572
	info@lonelyplanet.com
UK	Media Centre, 201 Wood Lane
	London W12 7TQ
	☎ 020 8433 1333 fax 020 8702 0112
	go@lonelyplanet.co.uk

This title was commissioned in Lonely Planet's London
office and produced by: **Commissioning Editor**
Paula Hardy **Coordinating Editor** Barbara Delissen
Coordinating Cartographer Brendan Streager
Layout Designer Carlos Solarte **Assisting Editors**
Chris Girdler, Anne Mulvaney **Managing Editor** Imogen
Bannister **Managing Cartographer** Alison Lyall **Cover
Researcher** Naomi Parker, lonelyplanetimages.com
Project Manager Annelies Mertens **Managing Layout
Designer** Celia Wood **Thanks to** Melanie Dankel, Frank
Deim, Craig Kilburn, Indra Kilfoyle, Lisa Knights, Jo Potts,
Kalya Ryan, Lyahna Spencer, Laura Stansfeld, Glenn
Vanderknijff, Aude Vauconsant

ISBN 978 1 74179 712 1

10 9 8 7 6 5 4 3
Printed in China.

Acknowledgement Venice Vaporetto map © Actv SpA 2008

HOW TO USE THIS BOOK
Colour-Coding & Maps

Colour-coding is used for symbols on maps and
in the text that they relate to (eg all eating
venues on the maps and in the text are given
a green knife and fork symbol). Each *sestiere*
(neighbourhood) also gets its own colour, and
this is used down the edge of the page and
throughout that neighbourhood section.

Send us your feedback We love to hear from
readers — your comments help make our books better. We read every word you send us, and we always
guarantee that your feedback goes straight to the
appropriate authors. The most useful submissions are
rewarded with a free book. To send us your updates
and find out about Lonely Planet events, newsletters
and travel news visit our award-winning website:
lonelyplanet.com/contact

Note: We may edit, reproduce and incorporate
your comments in Lonely Planet products such as
guidebooks, websites and digital products, so let us
know if you don't want your comments reproduced or
your name acknowledged. For a copy of our privacy
policy visit *lonelyplanet.com/privacy*.

MIX
Paper from
responsible sources
FSC™ C021741
www.fsc.org

ALISON BING

When not scribbling notes in church pews and
methodically eating her way across Venice, Alison
contributes to Lonely Planet's *Italy*, *Milan* and
Tuscany & Umbria guides, as well as architecture,
food and art glossies such as *Architectural Record*,
Cooking Light and Italy's *Flash Art*. Currently she
divides her time between San Francisco and a
hilltop town on the border of Lazio and Tuscany
with partner (and fellow Slow Food member)
Marco Flavio Marinucci. Alison holds a bachelor's
degree in art history and a masters degree from
the Fletcher School of Law and Diplomacy, a
joint program between Tufts and Harvard Universities, but she regularly
undermines these perfectly respectable diplomatic credentials with opin
ionated culture commentary for newspapers, magazines and radio.

ALISON'S THANKS

Complimenti e grazie tanto a Davide Amadio, Jane and Luigi Caporal, Sigfrido Cipolato, Rosanna Corró, Giovanni d'Este, Francesca Forni, Francesco
and Matteo Pinto, and Cristina Bottero of the Venice Tourism Office. *Mille
grazie e baccione alla mia famiglia a Roma e* Stateside, the Bings, Ferrys,
Marinuccis and Cockrells; *come sempre* to fearless leader and fellow travel-
ler Paula Hardy; a thunderous *brava!* for dauntless editors Sasha Baskett
and Jo Potts and *bravo!* to *calle* cartographer Herman So; *ma sopra tutto a*
Marco Flavio Marinucci, who makes every discovery worthwhile.

   This book is dedicated to *voáltri venexiani,* who keep the city and its
spirits afloat.

Our readers Many thanks to the travellers who wrote to us with helpful hints, useful advice and interesting anecdotes: Duncan Bullimore, Karin Godvliet, Harlene Griffiths, Kelvin Hayes, Waldo Martin, Peter Rothstein, René Seindal, Georg Sengstschmid.

Photographs p52, p76, p93, p116, p129, p143 by Alison Bing; p12, p16 The Bridgeman Art Library, p17 David Kilpatrick/ Alamy; p26 Christine Widdall/Alamy; p134 Travelshots.com/Alamy; p130 Marco Ferracuti/Figli delle Stelle; p18 Dan Kitwood/ Getty Images; p29 Christophe Simon/AFP/Getty Images; p27 Mark Edward Smith/Photolibrary. All other photographs by Lonely Planet Images, and by Krzysztof Dydynski except p64 Glenn Beanland; p68, p160 Diana Mayfield; p30 Roberto Soncin Gerometta; p102 John Hay; p156 Karl Blackwell; p20, p126 Richard Cummins; p144 Greg Elms; p138 Jon Davison; p31 Holger Leue; p25 David Tomlinson; p21, p32 (top left), p34, p118, p163 Brent Winebrenner; p8, p14, p19, p27, p57, p99 Juliet Coombe. **Cover photograph** Venice, San Giorgio Maggiore, Gondola and Bacino San Marco, Basilica by Andrea Palladio architect.

All images are copyright of the photographers unless otherwise indicated. Many of the images in this guide are available for licensing from **Lonely Planet Images:** www.lonelyplanetimages.com.

Bow to the inevitable and take a gorgeous gondola ride (p175)

CONTENTS

THIS IS VENICE

As you approach the portals of the Basilica di San Marco, you feel a buzz surge through the crowd. A moment ago, you were a motley group of tourists, art students and the occasional nun – now you're ensemble players in the epic drama that is Venice.

Yet Venice isn't a one-stage venue. The dazzling pageantry continues at I Frari, Gallerie dell'Accademia, Scuola Grande di San Rocco and, of course, Teatro La Fenice. And if you think your walk-on part at these attractions is exhilarating, wait until you step backstage – which is never more than a *sotoportego* (passageway) away. In narrow *calli* (streets) off the thoroughfares to San Marco, you'll glimpse the behind-the-scenes creativity that keeps the whole production afloat: artisans at work in their studios, cooks whipping up four-star *cicheti* (Venetian tapas) on single-burner hotplates, musicians lugging 18th-century cellos to chamber-music practice. Here the volume is turned down, and you can hear the muffled sounds of intermission – neighbours kissing hello and Veronese spaniels trotting over footbridges.

But haven't Venetians heard their city is sinking? Absolutely – and true to form, they're staging a creative comeback. Venice has already survived plague, invasion and floods; under threat of imminent destruction, Venetians painted masterpieces, invented new architecture styles and created new musical genres. But rising tides are one thing, cruise ships are another. Millions of visitors annually disembark with just three hours to tour Venice, and if each day tripper asked one local for directions to San Marco, every Venetian would hear the question repeated 333 times a year.

This is where you come in. With your excellent map and insider info, ask questions Venetians actually enjoy answering. What's the best Venetian dish? How about those Venice Film Festival winners? And the most revealing question of all: what's new? Already there are new twists on baroque music, new galleries in ancient warehouses and new hotels in Palladian cloisters. Your timing is perfect – Venice's next act is just beginning.

Top left Gain a new perspective on the Campanile di San Marco (p44) **Top right** Wooden, me? Try to outstare the mannequins at Fiorella Gallery (p49) **Bottom** Gondolas? Check. Stripy shirt? Check. It must be Venice.

Morning mists shroud Piazza San Marco (p40)

>1 BASILICA DI SAN MARCO

PREPARE TO BE WOWED BY THE BASILICA DI SAN MARCO

The burning question isn't *if* you should see Venice's jewel of a cathedral, but when. Morning mystics insist you must arrive when millions of sunlit tesserae emit an otherworldly glow, causing jaws to drop to the semiprecious-stone floors. Sunset romantics lobby you to linger in the Piazza San Marco, waiting for the fading sun to shatter portal mosaics into golden shards as the Caffè Florian house band strikes up the tango. Our advice? Go now, and go often. With millennium-old special-effects wizardry that puts modern Hollywood to shame, the basilica is set to dazzle morning to night, inside and out.

This landmark was inspired by religious larceny in 828, when Venetian merchants smuggled the corpse of St Mark out of Egypt. Venice already had all the makings of a global trading centre – plenty of ports, a defendable position against Charlemagne and the Huns, a patron saint to oversee transactions – but there was no glorious landmark to fix Venice's place on the world map. And so the city summoned the best artisans from Byzantium and beyond to enshrine both the relic and Venice's trading prowess in one unmistakable monument.

But there remained the small matter of construction. The usual medieval setbacks of riots and fires thrice destroyed exterior mosaics and weakened the underlying structure. As ceilings drooped and tastes changed, Jacopo Sansovino and other church architects grafted on

TOP FIVE SAN MARCO MUST SEES

> Cupola of the Ascension – the golden central dome is truly uplifting, with angels swirling overhead and a dreamy-eyed St Mark on the pendentive (dome support).
> Pala d'Oro – minutely worked enamel portraits of apostles in superhero capes outshine the 2000 gemstones on this priceless altarpiece.
> Dome of Genesis – created 650 years before abstract art and hip hop, these medieval mosaics show the separation of sky and water, and angels busting dance moves.
> Pavimenti – prepare to be floored by the dizzying optical effects of polychrome stone mosaics.
> Loggia dei Cavalli – bronze horses leap off the balcony over Piazza San Marco.

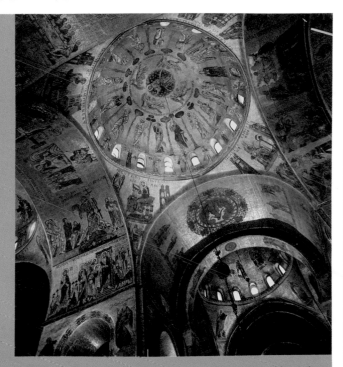

supports, Gothic arches and every type of polychrome marble available for purchase or pillage. Occasionally higher purpose got clouded over by construction dust: St Mark's bones were misplaced twice.

Give or take a holy tibia, Venice's transition from backwater upstart to sophisticated cosmopolitan capital was successfully completed by the 18th century. Today, even during the high tides that wash over the sinking piazza, San Marco still sets the high-water mark for architectural amazement.

See p41 for more information.

>2 GALLERIE DELL'ACCADEMIA

HEAD TO THE ACCADEMIA FOR ART THAT'S CAUSED CENTURIES OF SCANDAL AND SENSATION

Somewhere in the queue to enter the Accademia, you may grumpily wonder if the wait is worthwhile. But when the masses of students part to reveal Andrea Mantegna's 1466 haughtily handsome *St George* or Rosalba Carriera's brutally honest self-portrait from 1730, you'll get the thrill of locking eyes with a major celebrity across a crowded room.

The Accademia is hardly strictly academic – it also holds all the unforgettable characters, tall tales, murderous intrigue and juicy scandals that could be expected from the most extreme Venetian dinner parties. Giovanni Bellini's gorgeous Madonna is haloed by red cher-

TOP FIVE PORTRAITS THAT LOOK ALIVE
> Giorgione's *Old Woman*
> Hans Memling's *Portrait of a Young Man*
> Gentile Bellini's *Blessed Lorenzo Giustinian*
> Giambattista Piazzetta's *Fortune-Teller*
> Lorenzo Lotto's *Portrait of a Young Scholar*

ubs glowing like XXX neon signs, while a bejewelled beauty in the corner steals the Madonna's thunder in Titian's *Mary's Presentation in the Temple*. Tintoretto's Old Testament account of God's creation of the animals is suspiciously Venetian, with its spotlighted lions (the symbol of St Mark) and mutant lagoon fish that would definitely be sold at a discount at the Pescheria. Giambattista Tiepolo's *Miracle of the Bronze Serpent* is cracked from when it was hastily rolled up by creeped-out viewers, but for sheer, shimmering gore, there's no topping Vittore Carpaccio's *Crucifixion and Glorification of the Ten Thousand Martyrs of Mount Ararat*. Suffice to say, Harry's Bar was quite correct in naming a dish of bloody raw beef after this painter.

But the most controversial scene stealer is Paolo Veronese's *Feast in the House of Levi* (pictured above), which was called *The Last Supper* until Inquisition leaders condemned Veronese for showing drunkards, dwarves, dogs and even Reformation-minded Germans cavorting amid the apostles. Veronese refused to change a thing besides the title, and Venice stood by this act of artistic defiance. Follow the exchanges, gestures and eye contact among the characters here, and you'll notice that not one Moorish trader, stumbling servant, gambler or bright-eyed lapdog could have been painted over without losing an essential piece of the puzzle – and not coincidentally, the same can be said of Venice.

See p112 for more information.

VEN

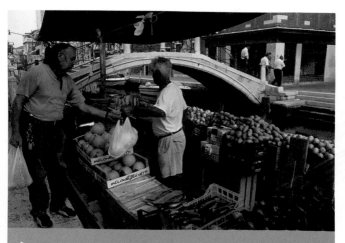

>3 OPEN-AIR MARKETS

FIND ALL THE FIXINGS FOR VENICE'S SIGNATURE DISHES AT THE CITY'S MARKETS

Cutting-edge restaurants worldwide are catching on to something Venetians have known for 600 years: food tastes better when it's fresh, seasonal and local. The Pescheria (Fish Market; p94) is any foodie's first stop in Venice – especially for *moscardino* (baby octopus), crabs ranging from tiny *moeche* (soft-shell crabs) to *granseole* (spider crabs), and *seppie* (squid) of all sizes.

Compared to the tame specimens you'd find at your average supermarket, the indigenous Veneto fare at the Rialto produce markets (p94) and on canalside stalls (boxed text, p95) looks like it just landed from another planet. Tiny purplish *castraure* (baby artichokes) could be shrunken alien heads, white Bassano asparagus is eerily spectral and red radicchio di Treviso looks like a mutant flower from Mars. Even familiar food goes wild here: suggestively shaped tomatoes and red capsicum seem very fresh indeed, and those saucy little strawberries could make grown men cry.

>4 TINTORETTO

CHASE LIGHTNING FLASHES OF INSIGHT THROUGH TINTORETTO'S STORMY SCENES

Lightning bolts can scarcely keep up with Tintoretto's loaded paint-brush as it streaks across familiar scenes, illuminating them from within. His subject matter was typically dictated by his patrons – biblical scenes, mythical allegories, odes to the greats of Venice – but he made them seem new with his careful spotlighting, stormy backdrops and vertigo-inducing perspective.

A crash course in Tintoretto begins at his preserved *bottega* (work-shop; p80), then nips around the corner to Chiesa della Madonna dell'Orto (p74), his parish church and the serene backdrop for his action-packed 1546 *Last Judgment*. True-blue Venetian that he is, Tin-toretto shows the final purge as a teal tidal wave, with lost souls vainly trying to hold it back like human MOSE barriers (seeboxed text, p172). The riveting image of a dive-bombing angel swooping in to save one last person was reprised by Tintoretto in the upper floor of Scuola Grande di San Rocco (pictured above; p86), where he spent some 15 years creating works for the patron saint of plague victims. His biblical scenes here read like a graphic novel, with backdrops fading to black to capture the drama of Jesus' final days and the Black Death, the dark-ness lightened only by the artist's streaky white rays of hope.

>5 TITIAN

TRAIL TITIAN ACROSS TOWN FROM MASTERPIECE TO MASTERPIECE

In other cities you might actually have to search to find artistic inspiration, but in Venice you can just follow the footbridges to the first, last and best paintings by the master of the red-hot moment. At the Santa Maria della Salute (p109), you'll notice Titian started out a measured, methodical painter in his 1510 *St Marco Enthroned*, although his brushwork was already loose enough and vermillion vibrant enough to add dynamism to a straightforward scene. But after seeing Michelangelo's writhing *Last Judgment* Titian let it rip, and his expressive urgency is palpable in his final 1576 *Pietà*, where he smeared paint onto the canvas with his bare hands.

But even for a man of many masterpieces, Titian's *Madonna of the Assumption* at I Frari (pictured above; p84) is an astonishing accomplishment. Titian has captured the instant when the Madonna has risen beyond the grasp of the lowly mortals below, with the angels putting their backs into the final push. This altarpiece seems to fill the nave with the radiant warmth of the Madonna's red robes, and that pale wrist revealed by a slipping sleeve has been known to get priests too hot and bothered to pray.

>6 LA BIENNALE DI VENEZIA

GLIMPSE THE FUTURE AT LA BIENNALE DI VENEZIA

Seems like every German city holds a contemporary-art biennale these days - but when connoisseurs talk about *the* Biennale, they still mean Venice. Started in 1895 as a corrective to the brutality of the Industrial Revolution and to reassert Venice's role as a tastemaker, the Biennale was initially a conservative institution. A grand pavilion provided an inoffensive take on Italy's latest artistic achievements – mainly lovely ladies, pretty flowers and lovely ladies wearing pretty flowers. Other nations were granted pavilions in 1907, but the Biennale foundation retained control, even removing a Picasso from the Spanish Pavilion in 1910 so as not to shock the public with modernity.

Then one world war after another erupted, making such delicacy seem terribly antiquated. The post-WWI Biennale boldly exhibited works by Amedeo Modigliani, whose abstract blank-eyed women were hotly debated. Venice wasn't instantly convinced by modernism, but it did discover an appetite for artistic controversy, as new pavilions for Korea, Japan and Canada highlighted avant-garde art and architecture. Both highly anticipated events spur satellite shows across the city, with the Biennale's autumn showcase for avant-garde architecture (in even-numbered years) held in the historic Arsenale and the summer art extravaganza (odd-numbered years) packing Biennale pavilions with masterworks by 90 artists.

See p29 and p59 for more.

>7 VENICE FILM FESTIVAL

WATCH THE STARS ALIGN AT THE VENICE FILM FESTIVAL

When the Venice Biennale announced its first film showcase in 1932, the scandal threatened to sink Venice. 'What kind of a city would risk its reputation on popular entertainment?' sniffed Cannes, New York and Telluride. The Oscars were still being held in the Fiesta Room at Hollywood's Ambassador Hotel (seating capacity: 900), so no one imagined that the far-flung Lido would be swamped with filmgoers. But once Joan Crawford and Clark Gable hit the red carpet, and 25,000 people showed up for screenings, the festival and its Golden Lion awards proved to be a winning formula of art and celebrity.

Never an indie-film showcase, the Venice Film Festival has gained a reputation as the film festival that rewards directors who should have won Oscars on sheer creative merit. Directors featured at Venice include David Fincher *(Fight Club)*, Spike Jonze *(Being John Malkovich)*, Antoine Fuqua *(Training Day)* and Ang Lee *(Brokeback Mountain)*, as well as perennial favourites Woody Allen, Takeshi Kitano, Martin Scorsese and Zhang Yimou.

See p29 and p135 for more.

>8 THE GHETTO

EXPLORE THE GHETTO, THE NEIGHBOURHOOD THAT LAUNCHED A RENAISSANCE

Standing in the Ghetto's lopsided main square (p71), surrounded by ramshackle buildings, you'd never guess that this was the heart of an empire. In accordance with the Venetian Republic's 1516 decree, by day Jewish lenders funded Venice's commercial enterprises, while by night and on Christian holidays they were restricted to the gated Ghetto Nuovo.

When Jewish merchants fled to Venice from the Spanish Inquisition in 1541, there was no place for them to go but up. Additional storeys on existing buildings in the Ghetto housed new arrivals and synagogues, while across town the Renaissance was advanced by Jewish lenders and Jewish artisans, filling palaces and churches with priceless treasures. But through papal restrictions and plague, the Ghetto was reduced to 3000 inhabitants by 1670.

After Napoleon lifted restrictions in 1797, Ghetto residents gained standing as Venetian citizens. But Mussolini's 1938 race laws were throwbacks to the 16th century, and in 1943 most of the 1670 Jews in Venice were rounded up and sent to concentration camps; only 37 returned. Venice's Jewish community now numbers around 420, but children playing tag in the *campo* (square) show there's still life left in the Ghetto. To explore some of the Ghetto's seven synagogues (pictured above), book a tour with the Museo Ebraico di Venezia (p74).

>9 NIGHT AT THE OPERA
GET A PERFORMANCE HIGH AT TEATRO LA FENICE

No matter what's on the bill at Teatro La Fenice (p57), there's bound to be drama. Before the doors open, the buzz begins at cafes around the piazza, where tousled artistes and coiffed socialites gather to toss back prosecco with an espresso chaser. Once the crowd heads inside the theatre, wraps are shed in lower-tier boxes to reveal jewels and Murano-glass baubles, while in the cheap seats of the top-tier *loggie* (balconies), the *loggione* (opera critics) predict which singers will be in good voice and which understudies may be due for a promotion. Architecture aficionados find other subjects to argue about -- namely whether the historically accurate reconstruction after the 1996 fire was worth €90 million, or whether the baroque 'inverted-wedding-cake' style should have been modernised by architect Gae Aulenti as originally planned. But when the overture begins, all voices hush and the air turns electric with anticipation. No one wants to miss a note of a performance that could compare with historic premieres by Stravinsky, Rossini, Prokofiev, Britten and, of course, Giuseppe Verdi.

>10 BEHIND THE SCENES

VEER OFF THE TOURIST TRACK TO HIDDEN GEMS

Pity the cruise-ship crowds are dropped off at San Marco with a mere three hours to take in Venice. That's about enough time for one long gasp at the show-stopper that is Piazza San Marco, but not nearly enough to see what else Venice is hiding behind its Moorish Gothic portals. For those who stray off the tourist trail, yellow signs helpfully point the way back to San Marco from the obvious landmarks of the Rialto, Gallerie dell'Accademia and train station, bypassing a maze of *calli* (streets), *sotoportegi* (passageways) and canals. But here's the secret to any great Venetian adventure: *ignore those signs*.

With an adventurous spirit and a decent map, you can plunge into Venice's labyrinth, discovering the city behind the Grand Canal facades. Dine like a local in hidden *cortili* (courtyards), stay overnight in a *palazzo* (palace or mansion) and wake up to the sound of gondolieri calling 'Oooooooeeeeeeee!' as they manoeuvre long boats around blind corners. From where you stand at a local *bacaro* (bar), you can watch the day trippers thunder past to their trains, planes and buses, and simply drink in Venice.

>11 CA' REZZONICO

SEE HOW VENICE'S SPIRITS SOARED, EVEN AS ITS POWER WANED, AT CA' REZZONICO

Saying that Venice's glory days ended with the 16th century is like saying the city peaked while a teenager – and it completely overlooks the splendours of Ca' Rezzonico, aka the Museum of 18th-Century Venice.

For all its breezy gorgeousness, the Ca' Rezzonico's wits are razor sharp. Airy and light without seeming frou-frou, the Ca' Rezzonico is a Baldassare Longhena–designed palace that was just right for its time. Giambattista Tiepolo covered the Ca' Rezzonico's ceilings with shamelessly flattering paintings, showing Ludovico Rezzonico and his bride surrounded by Fame, Wisdom and Merit – but these trompe l'œil domes are so clever, colourful and overtly theatrical that it seems Tiepolo was just gleefully showing off.

By the 18th century, Venice had lived through plague, defended itself against Turkish invasion and seen its world-domination ambitions dashed – but it was determined to make light of a dire situation, and its tragicomic tendencies are captured in the art of the period. An entire drawing room at the Ca' Rezzonico is dedicated to Pietro Longhi's drawing-room satires, including *The Morning Chocolate* (1775), which shows fashionable Venetians bingeing on trendy cocoa and doughnuts at the risk of popping their waistcoat buttons or upsetting a disapproving lapdog. Rosalba Carriera captures her sitters' every quirk in her pastel portraits, and their sly smirks make them look like the life of any 18th-century party.

See p109 for more information.

>12 GOING FOR BAROQUE

HEAR BAROQUE LIKE NEVER BEFORE

When pop seems overplayed and jazz standards a little too standard, Venice offers an alternative: baroque. Venetian baroque was the rebel music of its day, openly defying edicts from Rome that set down which instruments could accompany sermons, and what kinds of rhythms and melodies were suitable for uplifting morals. But Venetians kept on playing stringed instruments in churches, singing along to bawdy *opera buffa* (comic opera), and capturing the full range of human experience in sensual, explosive compositions. Modern misconceptions that baroque is simply a nice accompaniment to wedding ceremonies are smashed by baroque 'early-music' ensembles such as Venice Baroque Opera, which commands international followings with its original 18th-century instruments and shockingly contemporary interpretations of baroque pieces.

Venice's best-loved composer is Vivaldi, and though his *Four Seasons* may be instantly recognisable from hotel-lobby muzak and mobile-phone ringtones, you haven't really heard summer lightning strike and spring threaten to flood the room until you've heard Vivaldi played by Interpreti Veneziani (p56). Also look for programs featuring Venetian baroque composer Tomaso Albinoni.

Finally, make sure you consider the venue – any baroque performance in the Casa di Goldoni (p84), the Ca' Rezzonico (p109) or the Ospedaletto (pictured above) will transport you to the 18th century in one movement, and catapult you into the 21st in the next.

HIGHLIGHTS

>13 TORCELLO & BURANO

EXPLORE THE OUTER LIMITS OF THE LAGOON ON TORCELLO AND BURANO

Once you've wrapped your head around the improbable existence of Venice – who builds a city on a silty lagoon? – Burano (p140) and Torcello (p144) defy your imagination all over again.

Photographers in inspiration overdrive dash off the ferry into Burano's backstreets, snapping away at turquoise window boxes filled with red geraniums, and green stockings hung out to dry between pink and orange houses. Either there is some law requiring locals to choose contrasting paint schemes and complementary-colour skivvies, or Burano is naturally the most artistically inclined fishing village in the Mediterranean basin.

On the pastoral island of Torcello, sheep easily outnumber the 20 or so human residents. But this bucolic backwater was once a Byzantine metropolis of 20,000 – and it has the stunning mosaics to prove it. In a scene from the Last Judgment in Torcello's Cattedrale di Santa Maria Assunta, a band of holy avengers arrives to save the day: Jesus breaks down the doors of hell while a sea nymph representing the Adriatic ushers souls lost at sea towards Peter, who's jangling the keys to Paradise like God's own bouncer. These Byzantine mosaics are often compared to those in the Basilica di San Marco but, if you want an epic adventure, Torcello is worth the trip.

>14 DUCAL PALACE

TAKE A WALK TO THE DOGI'S DARK SIDE IN THE DUCAL PALACE

From the outside, the restored Ducal Palace is all elegant brickwork and graceful Gothic colonnades, but the inside of the *palazzo* reveals a darker side to the dogi (Venice's leaders). Right behind a grand salon festooned with cherubim and Paolo Veronese's allegories of Virtue conquering Vice lie the cramped secret headquarters of the shadowy Consiglio dei Dieci (Council of Ten), Venice's version of the CIA. Upstairs was the Piombi, the dread attic prison where Casanova was sentenced to five years' confinement on charges of corrupting nuns and spreading Freemasonry.

Casanova charmed his way past the guards in 1757, and you too can plot your escape from the Piombi on the fascinating Itinerari Segreti (Secret Passageways) tour. This tour leads you through the Consiglio dei Dieci's administrative offices to a windowless room with a single rope: the dogi's torture chamber. To Venice's credit, the room was largely disused by the 17th century – but the same cannot be said for the studded cells where the accused awaited trial. Renaissance Venice was no place for rebels: anyone who dared question the rosy depiction of Venetian government on view downstairs just might be taken upstairs.

See p45 for more information.

HIGHLIGHTS

>15 PUNTA DELLA DOGANA
UNCANNY CONTEMPORARY ART IN AN UNCUSTOMARY SETTING

Warehouses make the coolest art spaces – especially when they're over 300 years old. When French magnate François Pinault's collection of contemporary art proved too big for his Palazzo Grassi (p47), Pinault again collaborated with minimalist architect Tadao Ando to repurpose a 17th-century wedge-shaped customs warehouse into a cutting-edge showcase, fit for major statements by controversial international art stars. Three years and €20 million later, the galleries await your inspection. Pass through a haunting Feliz Gonzales-Torres blood-red bead curtain and you'll enter a skylit gallery illuminating a Maurizio Cattelan horse's rear disappearing into the brick wall, above candy-coloured pedestals Rachel Whiteread cast from the undersides of lecture chairs. There's plenty more to fascinate and offend – possibly both, if you catch Dinos and Jake Chapman's version of the nine circles of hell populated by 30,000 Nazi figurines. Other pieces are apparently too enchanting for their own good: in a darkened gallery adjoining the museum's bookstore/cafe, Mike Kelley's superhero hometowns gave off such a transfixing glow that more than one dazzled visitor has bumped into or tried to pocket them. For more on this place, see p114.

>VENICE DIARY

Three rules for revellers are posted at vaporetto (city-ferry) stops: no littering in the canals, no defacing historic buildings and no strutting about bare breasted. The fact that Venice feels obliged to post that last regulation shows that opportunities for, erm, self-expression don't begin and end with Carnevale. Whether you like to spend your downtime getting arty, sweaty, mystical or all of the above, Venice has you covered, with Biennales, marathons and weddings to the sea. A warning, though: this town seems determined to see you dunked. Many festivals entail crossing makeshift pontoon bridges or rowing while standing up — and boozing canalside has obvious risks.

Don't miss the spectacular fireworks at the Festa ∧ l Redentore (p29)

FEBRUARY

Carnevale

www.carnevale.venezia.it

Even Napoleon couldn't stop Venice's signature event. Before Lent begins, masqueraders party in the streets — and occasionally fall into canals — in long-nosed masks and commedia dell'arte costumes. If your liver hurts and wig itches after 10 days, just imagine how you'd have felt in the 18th century, when the party lasted up to three months.

APRIL

Festa di San Marco

www.comune.venezia.it

Citizen Kane would appreciate the celebration of Venice's patron saint on 25 April — the recurring motif is a *bocolo* (rosebud). Venetian men carry roses in processions through Piazza San Marco, and give them to the women they love best.

Scare small children during Carnevale

TOP FIVE WAYS TO CELEBRATE CARNEVALE

> Slide tackle in knee britches at Calcio Storico, a fancy-dress football match in Piazza San Marco.
> Binge on *frittelle*, the rum-raisin doughnuts that are best eaten when still warm.
> Quadrille the night away at Teatro La Fenice's masked ball on the second Saturday of Carnevale (tickets start at €200; costume and dance classes not included).
> Watch the Grand Canal parade, where the floats actually float.
> Have a historically accurate blast, or DIY trying, by making your own costume and mastering the art of mask acting at Teatro Junghans (p131).

MAY

Vogalonga

www.turismovenezia.it

Not so much a race as a test of endurance, this 32km 'Long Row' starts with 1000 boats in front of the Ducal Palace, loops past Burano and Murano, and ends several boats shy of the starting number at Punta della Dogana.

Festa della Sensa

www.sevenonline.it/sensa

Venice loves its lagoon so much that it has renewed its vows to the water every year since AD 998. In the Sposalizio del Mar (Wedding to the Sea), the mayor tosses a gold ring in the waters near San Nicolò on the Lido.

JUNE

Venezia Suona

www.veneziasuona.it

Hear medieval *campi* (squares) and baroque *palazzi* (palaces or mansions) echo with the latest sounds from around the world.

La Biennale di Venezia

www.labiennale.org

In odd-numbered years the Art Biennale usually runs from June to November, and in even years the Architecture Biennale kicks off in September – but every summer there's also avant-garde dance, theatre, cinema and music. See p17.

JULY

Festa del Redentore

www.turismovenezia.it

Walk on water across the Canal della Giudecca to Il Redentore (p128) via a wobbly pontoon bridge on the third Saturday and Sunday in July. Join the floating picnic along the Zattere, and don't miss the fireworks.

AUGUST

Venice Film Festival

www.labiennale.org/en/cinema

The only thing hotter than Lido beaches in August is the red carpet at this star-studded event, which runs from the last weekend in August through the first week of September.

Star-gaze at the Venice Film Festival

SEPTEMBER

Venice International Festival of Contemporary Music

www.labiennale.org

Held since 1930, this has become the obsessive music lover's must-see program, premiering works by classical innovators Stravinsky and Prokofiev as well as leading international blues, electronica and flamenco artists. Performances are held in the last week of September in Arsenale warehouses.

Regata Storica

www.comune.venezia.it

Never mind who's winning, check out all the cool gear. At the Historical Regatta, 16th-century costumes, eight-oared gondolas and ceremonial barques all feature in a procession reenacting the arrival of the queen of Cyprus. Kids, women and gondolieri compete for boating bragging rights.

Regata di Burano

www.comune.venezia.it

The final grudge match of the regatta season, the Regata di Burano is the race where rowers either gloat over their definitive win or take consolation in plenty of local fish, polenta and white wine.

OCTOBER

Venice Marathon

www.venicemarathon.com

Six thousand runners work up a sweat over 42km of spectacular scenery, dashing along the River Brenta past Palladian villas before crossing into Venice and heading to Piazza San Marco via a 160m floating bridge. Mind your step...

NOVEMBER

Festa della Madonna della Salute

www.turismovenezia.it

If you'd survived plague and Austrian invasion, you'd throw a party too. Every 21 November since the 17th century, Venetians have crossed a pontoon bridge across the Grand Canal to give thanks at Chiesa di Santa Maria della Salute (p109) and splurge on sweets.

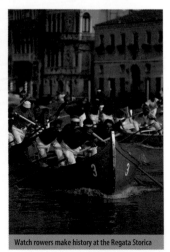

Watch rowers make history at the Regata Storica

>ITINERARIES

Every dog has its day in the piazzas of Venice

ITINERARIES

Why bother with time machines? A walk across Venice takes you from golden Byzantium to the Titian red Renaissance, from Vivaldi to video art. Immerse yourself in Venice's historical splendours, then step into the future with musical performances, contemporary art and artisanal handicrafts.

DAY ONE

Begin your day in prison on the Itinerari Segreti (Secret Passageways) tour of the Ducal Palace (p45), then make a break for Piazza San Marco. Lunch at Cavatappi (p51) will get you ready to take on the Gallerie dell'Accademia (p111), after which it's time for *aperitivi* and people-watching in Campo Santa Margherita. Grab a bite at Osteria alla Bifora (p123) before your Interpreti Veneziani concert (p56), held under the Carpaccio altarpiece in baroque Chiesa San Vidal. End the night gliding down the Grand Canal on a vaporetto (city ferry) or gondola.

DAY TWO

The Basilica di San Marco (p41) starts your day with a dazzle, and the art attack continues with modern art at Palazzo Grassi (p47), and Tintorettos and Canovas at Santo Stefano (p48). Your growling stomach will lead you across the Rialto to All'Arco (p91) for Francesco and Matteo's latest *cicheti* (Venetian tapas) creations, and to Gelateria San Stae (p105) for an ice cream. Make a cameo appearance in the costume drama of the museum of textiles at Palazzo Mocenigo (p102), then get lost in the former red-light district near Ponte delle Tette (p85) en route to Titian's masterpiece at I Frari (p84). Dine at Enoteca ai Artisti (p119), but chase that amarone with an espresso – tonight's entertainment is a performance at Teatro La Fenice (p57).

DAY THREE

Andrea Palladio's white Chiesa di San Giorgio Maggiore (p126) is beautifully blinding as you approach by vaporetto. Check out the Tintorettos by the altar, then nip around the back to see contemporary art at Fondazione Giorgio Cini (p127). Catch another vaporetto to lunch at I Figli delle Stelle (p130), then cover the waterfront from Il Redentore (p128) to Fortuny

---

Top left Get your daily exercise while exploring Venice's hidden bridges and passageways **Top right** Sigh over the stunning Ponte dei Sospiri (p45) **Bottom** Cruisin' down the river: classic Venetian transport, classic Venetian view

Tessuti Artistici (p128). Ride the vaporetto to Dorsoduro to pay respects to Peggy Guggenheim (p113), discover wall-to-wall Paolo Veronese paintings in Chiesa di San Sebastian (p109) and slurp Amalfi lemon gelato at Grom (p119). After you brave Tintoretto's tempests inside Scuola Grande di San Rocco (p86), window-shop your way to happy hour at Al Mercà (p96) and a Rialto bridge sunset (p86).

RAINY DAY

Skip the long, wet lines at the Gallerie dell'Accademia and Basilica di San Marco, and head to I Frari (p84) to bask in the glow of Titian's *Madonna of the Ascension*. Duck into the Scuola Grande di San Rocco (p86), where Tintoretto's stormy canvases make Venetian weather seem balmy, then warm up afterwards with prosecco and polenta at ImprontaCafé (p120). At the nearby Scuola Grande dei Carmini (p114), pass cloudy grey paintings downstairs and head up Baldassare Longhena's stairway to heaven to find the silver lining: Giambattista Tiepolo's *Virtues* ceiling. Blue skies are ahead at Ca' Rezzonico (p109), where Tiepolo's trompe l'œil sunlight brightens salon ceilings. Afterwards, pasta at Ristoteca Oniga (p121) will warm you from the inside out.

It might be *alta acqua* (high water) in Piazza San Marco (p40), but at least you can say you walked on water

FORWARD PLANNING

Three weeks before you go Book tickets online for opera at Teatro La Fenice (p57), movie premieres at the Venice Film Festival (p29) and the Itinerari Segreti (Secret Passageways) tour of the Ducal Palace (p45).

One week before you go Get your ticket online to the Art or Architecture Biennale (p29), call ahead for tickets to see Interpreti Veneziani (p56), book a lesson to learn to row like gondolieri (boxed text, p141), and skip the queues by booking tickets to the Gallerie dell'Accademia (p112) and various concerts at http://en.venezia.waf.it.

One day before you go Find out what live music, art openings and festivals are happening tomorrow in Venice at www.venezianews.it, www.veneziadavivere.com and www.aguestin venice.com; call to reserve a spot on Museo Ebraico di Venezia's tour (p75) of three to five of the historic synagogues in the Ghetto; call to book a restaurant for tomorrow; and pack your umbrella, swimsuit and powdered wig to cover all Venetian possibilities.

BEACH DAY

Hop on a vaporetto to the Lido and loll the day away on a beach chair, watching celebrities and ships drift past. Restless types can rent a bike at Lido on Bike (boxed text, p136) and pedal 1.5km north towards the Antico Cimitero Israelitico (p134), or cruise 6km down pine-shaded beachfront to the canal-lined town of Malamocco (p135). Unwind with happy-hour cocktails at the Colony Bar (p136), set on the verandah of historic Hotel des Bains, then grab dinner in the breezy garden at Trattoria La Favorita (p136). At night, catch a movie at the Venice Film Festival (p29) or Multisala Astra (p137), live music at Aurora Beach Club (p137) or beach DJ sets at Ultima Spiaggia di Pachuka (p137).

ON THE CHEAP

Wander past pavilions spanning modernist architecture movements in the gardens of the Biennale Internazionale d'Arte (p59), from the secessionist Austro-Hungarian Pavilion to the postindustrial Korea Pavilion. Stroll up the boardwalk to Basilica di San Marco (p41) to see priceless mosaics, gratis. Window-shop your way to the Rialto produce markets (p94) for fresh food and maybe even a free sample, then have a picnic at Campo San Giacometto. Head back across the Rialto to the Ghetto (p19) to spot rooftop synagogues and reflect on Venice's Jewish history before heading to Osteria agli Ormesini (p80) to see who'll buy you a drink. In summer, check out Campo San Polo (p97) for free outdoor music, movies and theatre.

Postcard perfect: the Ponte di Rialto (p86) is simply stunning

SESTIERI

For a city of islands, Venice isn't especially insular. Historically many Venetians rarely left their *sestieri* (neighbourhoods), and some were loath to even leave the island where they lived – but there's a certain logic to that inertia. Why would they need to leave when the world would come to them?

When Venetians such as Marco Polo did shove off from these shores, they returned with stories, ideas and booty from countries as far away as Mongolia. Even after its glory days as a global trading hub passed, Venice continued to attract poets, bon vivants and billionaire art collectors – anyone for whom beauty trumped convenience.

Even though it's now more accessible than ever, Venice remains a self-selecting city: only art and films that have proven themselves elsewhere make it to the Venice Biennale and the Venice Film Festival. But that doesn't make it snobby. The city welcomes anyone who manages to find their way to the outer reaches of Cannaregio, Castello, Santa Croce or Giudecca, or sticks around San Marco after the sightseers have cleared out.

Island fever isn't really a problem here. The *sestieri* are different enough that when restlessness begins to set in, you can just cross a couple of bridges or hop on a vaporetto (city ferry) to get a fresh perspective on the city. Overwhelmed by Byzantine glitz, Bellinis and shoe shopping in San Marco? Head to Santa Croce, where baroque edifices shelter modest cafes, wine comes straight from the cask, and talk revolves around boats and Berlusconi. For a change of pace from the industrial cool of Giudecca, hop on the vaporetto to Castello for a refreshing stretch of greenery. If you hit church overload in San Polo, you might explore synagogues in Cannaregio instead. When Lido beaches get crowded with fashionistas in giant hats, Dorsoduro's Zattere waterfront offers sun without the scene. To get away from it all, head for open waters and remote islands on the lagoon. It's all Venice, and it's all good.

>SAN MARCO

So many world-renowned attractions are packed into San Marco that some visitors never leave – while others are loath to visit, fearing a crush of day trippers and unappetising tourist menus. But it would be unfair to dismiss San Marco simply as a tourist trap. Piazza San Marco is gorgeously deserted by sunset, and just down San Marco's backstreets are authentic *osterie* (restaurant-bars) where you can eat and drink like a local. Besides, why deny yourself the pleasure of Teatro La Fenice, Basilica di San Marco, Palazzo Grassi and the Ducal Palace just to be contrarian? Go and judge for yourself whether these cultural landmarks earn their world-class reputations – but don't stop there. San Marco is packed with contemporary art galleries, chic boutiques and trendy *bacari* (bars). Rather than rest on its considerable laurels, San Marco keeps the inspiration coming.

SAN MARCO

👁 SEE
Ateneo di San Basso **1** G3
Basilica di San Marco **2** H4
Campanile di
  San Marco **3** G4
Caterina Tognon Arte
  Contemporanea **4** C6
Clock Tower **5** G4
Ducal Palace **6** H4
Galleria Traghetto **7** D5
Jarach Gallery **8** E4
La Galleria
  van der Koelen **9** D5
Museo Correr **10** F4
Museo Fortuny **11** C3
Palazzo Contarini
  del Bovolo **12** E4
Palazzo Grassi **13** A4
Santa Maria
  del Giglio **14** D5
Santo Stefano **15** C4

🛍 SHOP
Arcobaleno **16** B4
Arnoldo & Battois **17** E3
Ebrû **18** B4
Epicentro **19** F4
Esperienze **20** G3
Fiorella Gallery **21** B5
Gloria Astofolo **22** F4
La Pietra Filosofale **23** E4
Le Botteghe **24** F1
Libreria Studium **25** H3
Millevini **26** F1
Mondadori **27** F5
Ottica Carraro **28** D4
Venetia Studium **29** D5

🍽 EAT
Caffe Mandola **30** D4
Cavatappi **31** G3
Enoteca Al Volto **32** D3
Gelatoteca Suso **33** F1

Osteria Da Carla **34** F5
Sangal **35** F4
Vini da Arturo **36** D4

🍸 DRINK
B Bar **37** E5
Bacaro **38** F5
Harry's Bar **39** F5
I Rusteghi **40** F1
Teamo **41** C3
Torino@Notte **42** E3

⭐ PLAY
Caffè Florian 43 G5
Centrale 44 E4
Interpreti Veneziani 45 B5
Musica a Palazzo 46 C6
Teatro La Fenice 47 D4

Please see over for map

SEE

BASILICA DI SAN MARCO

☎ 041 5225205; www.basilicasanmarco
.it; Piazza San Marco; basilica free, Pala
d'Oro/Loggia dei Cavalli & Museum/
Treasury €2/4/3; ⏰ 9.45am-5pm Mon-
Sat, 2-4pm Sun Nov-Mar, to 5pm Apr-Oct;
🚤 San Marco, San Zaccaria, Vallaresso
If seen-it-all modern visitors gasp
to discover bright-eyed apostles
and luminous angels staring down
from San Marco's golden domes,
just imagine visitors' reactions in
the Middle Ages. At the time, most
medieval buildings in the region
were low wooden structures,
indoor lighting was dim and colour
pigments were rare imported

luxuries – and here was a soaring
stone structure with sunlight
bouncing off millions of tiny tesserae made from gold and crushed
semiprecious stones. Since San
Marco was officially the chapel of
the doge (Venice's leader), the dogi
took to displaying stolen treasures
in the basilica, including the gilded
bronze horses from Constantinople
that high-stepped over the central
portal. (These were later stolen by
Napoleon, but are now on display
inside; the ones over the portal on
the Loggia dei Cavalli are copies.)
Church authorities in Rome took a
dim view of Venice's tendency to
glorify itself and God in the same
breath, but Venice finished San

Get a horse's-eye view of the piazza from the Basilica di San Marco

Marco as it saw fit: the basilica's grand East-meets-West cosmopolitan style includes Eastern onion-bulb domes, a Greek cross layout, Gothic arches, and dizzying puzzlework floors made from Egyptian marble. The roped-off circuit of the church is free and takes about 15 minutes; going through twice is recommended to recover from the initial astonishment. The Loggia dei Cavalli is worth a look for its views over Piazza San Marco, but the alabaster chalices and icons in the Treasury can't quite compare to the exquisite enamel miniatures on the bejewelled Pala d'Oro altarpiece. Note that you'll need to be dressed modestly (ie knees and shoulders covered) to enter the basilica, and large bags must be left around the corner at **Ateneo di San Basso** (🕙 9.30am-5.30pm). See p10 for more information.

📷 CAMPANILE DI SAN MARCO
☎ 041 5225205; www.basilicasanmarco .it; Piazza San Marco; admission €8; 🕙 9am-7pm Apr-Jun & Oct, 9am-9pm Jul-Sep, 9.30am-3.45pm Nov-Mar; 🚏 San Marco, Vallaresso
There's no such thing as tall enough or skinny enough for this bell tower's critics, who for centuries have called the 99m brick tower squat and ungainly. But when the tower – which was raised in AD 888 and rebuilt in 1514 – unexpectedly collapsed in a heap

in 1902, city leaders rebuilt it exactly as it was. Fondness for the icon that served as the city's lighthouse trumped the objections of naysayers, who have to concede that the view from the top is breathtaking.

📷 CATERINA TOGNON ARTE CONTEMPORANEA
☎ 041 5207859; www.caterinatognon .com; Palazzo da Ponte, Calle delle Dose 2746; admission free; 🕙 3-7pm Wed-Sat; 🚏 Santa Maria del Giglio
Press the 'stART' doorbell on this 17th-century palace, and you'll be buzzed up to the 2nd-storey gallery and ahead of the art curve. Artists are encouraged to experiment with Venetian materials and ideas: Kiki Smith created Venetian glass vessels, while Richard Marquis designed colourful camouflage that allows battleships to enter stealth mode amid confetti showers and Murano glass showrooms.

📷 CLOCK TOWER
☎ 041 5209070; www.museicivicivenez iani.it; Piazza San Marco; guided tours adult/with Venice Card or St Mark's Museum Pass €12/7; 🕙 tour times (English) 10am & 11am Mon-Wed, 2pm & 3pm Thu-Sun; 🚏 San Marco, Vallaresso
Legend has it that the experts who invented the works of this astronomical clock were assassinated so that no other city could boast a similar engineering marvel. But

now visitors can see for themselves what makes this tower tick on special tours of the recently renovated monument. The terrace looks past the statues of the two Moors over Piazza San Marco, and the view is well worth the climb up the steep, claustrophobia-triggering spiral staircase. In the piazza, look up to see three kings and an angel emerge from the clock on Epiphany (6 January) and the Feast of the Ascension (second Sunday in May).

☑ DUCAL PALACE
☎ 041 2715911; www.museicivicivenez iani.it; Piazza San Marco 1; incl Museo Correr & 1 civic museum adult/student €13/7.50; ☉ 9am-7pm Apr-Oct, 9am-6pm Nov-Mar ; 🚢 San Marco, Vallaresso
All the show-stopping splendour and sinister intrigue of the Venetian Republic are captured in this one civic monument, which is best viewed on the riveting **Itinerari Segreti** (Secret Passageways; tour incl admission to Ducal Palace adult/student €16/10; ☉ tours 9.55am, 10.45am & 11.35am) tour.

Enter through the Gothic-colonnaded courtyard, climb the Scala dei Censori (Stairs of the Censors) and Sansovino's Scala d'Oro (Golden Staircase), and emerge into rooms covered with gorgeous propaganda: Tintoretto's depictions of Venice's virtues, Giambattista Tiepolo's *Venice Receiving the Gifts of the Sea from Neptune* and, finally, the Council Room designed by An-

drea Palladio, with Paolo Veronese's shamelessly flattering ceilings depicting the good government of the Republic. In the trial chambers of the Consiglieri dei Dieci (Council of Ten), Venice's dreaded secret service, you can see the slot where written denunciations were placed, as well as Veronese's paintings of Juno scattering her gifts on Venice. Behind the doge's throne in the cavernous Grand Council room (inaugurated in 1419) is a vision of Paradise by Tintoretto's son Domenico that's more politically correct than pretty, crammed with 500 portraits of prominent Venetians (and Tintoretto patrons). Downstairs are hellish scenes by the master of apocalyptic visions, Hieronymus Bosch. Across the Ponte dei Sospiri (Bridge of Sighs) are Venice's 16th-century Prigione Nuove (New Prisons), dank cells covered with graffiti and protestations of innocence. Emerge from the dark side of Venice into the sunlight, and admire the pinkish palace loggia graced with lacy 15th-century Gothic arches. See p25 for more.

☑ GALLERIA TRAGHETTO
☎ 041 5221188; www.galleriatraghet to.it, in Italian; Campo Santa Maria del Giglio 2543; admission free; ☉ 3-7pm Mon-Sat; 🚢 Santa Maria del Giglio
This gallery has gutsy shows of young Italian and international artists on the brink of breakthrough.

Look for Rome-based Serafino Maiorano's artfully blurred digital photographs, with bleeding reds that evoke the work of Vittore Carpaccio, and paintings by Lithuanian Andrius Zakarauskas, where history is cleverly reduced to saluting, finger pointing and other iconic gestures.

◉ JARACH GALLERY

☎ 041 5221938; www.jarachgallery .com; Campo San Fantin 1997; admission free; ⏱ 10am-2pm & 3-7.30pm Tue-Sat; 🚊 Santa Maria del Giglio

While diva Teatro La Fenice holds centre stage in this piazza, this contemporary-photography gallery waits in the wings. Both the gallery's location – through a shadowy *sotoportego* (passageway) – and program are big on quiet drama and mystery; Simone Bergantini recently showed eerie photos of abandoned dresses and spectral garbage bags casting film-noir shadows.

◉ LA GALLERIA VAN DER KOELEN

☎ 041 5207415; www.galerie.vander koelen.de; Ramo Primo dei Calegheri 2566; admission free; ⏱ 10am-12.30pm & 3.30-6.30pm Mon-Sat; 🚊 Santa Maria del Giglio

Keeping a low profile behind the loud, proud La Fenice, and contrasting with the onslaught of colour and drama that is the Gallerie dell'Accademia, La Galleria is the eye in the centre of Venice's aesthetic storm. A recent show featured Günther Uecker's delicately brutal embossed-paper nails and detailed drawings of glass shards.

◉ MUSEO CORRER

☎ 041 2405211; www.museicivicivenez iani.it; Piazza San Marco 52; adult/student incl Ducal Palace & 1 civic museum €13/7.50; ⏱ 9am-7pm Apr-Oct, 10am-5pm Nov-Mar, ticket office closes 1 hr before museum; 🚊 San Marco, Vallaresso

Snicker if you must at his oversized hats and undersized beds, but Napoleon knew something about organisation, both military and architectural. Never mind that there was a church on the west end of Piazza San Marco: Napoleon razed the place to make room for a grand ballroom. Today the Museo Correr unifies the 1st and 2nd floors of the arcade overlooking the piazza, leading through Graeco-Roman statuary and splendid medieval paintings, and culminating in Venice's crowning glory: the Libreria Nazionale Marciana's 16th-century reading room, with representations of wisdom by Veronese and Titian. Don't miss the Caffè dell'Arte, covered in baroque grotesques of griffins and other beasties, and ideal for a €4 glass of Veneto merlot served with views of San Marco worthy of an emperor.

MUSEO FORTUNY

☎ 041 5200995; www.museicivicivenez iani.it; Campo San Beneto 3958; adult/student or with St Mark's Museum Pass €9/6; ☷ 10am-6pm Wed-Mon, ticket office closes 1 hr before museum; ⚎ Sant'Angelo

An eccentric for the ages and truly avant-garde, Spanish designer Mariano Fortuny y Madrazo loosened Victorian corsets with free-flowing Grecian dresses that drew bohemian devotees such as Isadora Duncan to his Gothic showroom. The rotating exhibitions are of variable interest, but the permanent draws are Moorish-deco chandeliers, salons sumptuously swagged with Fortuny's printed silks, and original Fortuny silk Delphos dresses alongside portraits of daringly bare Victorian ladies.

PALAZZO CONTARINI DEL BOVOLO

☎ 041 5322920; Calle Contarini del Bovolo 4299; courtyard free; ☷ 10am-6pm; ⚎ Rialto

Never mind that you can't peek inside the 15th-century *palazzo* (palace or mansion), or that the *bovolo* (snail-shell) staircase, wrapped in brick and decorated with white cutaway archways, is closed for restoration – the courtyard offers the best view of this jewel of Renaissance architecture.

PALAZZO GRASSI

☎ 199 139139; www.palazzograssi.it; Campo San Samuele 3231; adult/student & senior €15/10, with Punta della Dogana €20/14; ☷ 10am-7pm Wed-Mon; ⚎ San Samuele

Giorgio Masari's 1749 neoclassical palace became a glorious anachronism in 2006, when billionaire art collector François Pinault retrofitted it to showcase his contemporary art collection with minimalist architect Tadao Ando. Collection highlights include Takashi Murakami's smiling Superflat daisies, Raymond Pettibon's poetically captioned cartoons ('I curse the happy for whom the unhappy is only a spectacle') and Barbara Kruger's maxims ('We are astonishingly lifelike'). The Grassi's Grand Canal pier sculptures shock unsuspecting gondola-riders, and even its cafe is a rotating art installation.

SANTA MARIA DEL GIGLIO

Campo di Santa Maria Zobenigo 2543; admission €3, with Chorus pass free; ☷ 10am-5pm Mon-Sat; ⚎ Santa Maria del Giglio

A small baroque neighbourhood church from the outside, Santa Maria del Giglio is a small wonder inside, with a 10th-century

Byzantine layout and intriguing works by three European masters.

Hiding behind the altar is Veronese's *Madonna with Child,* with Tintoretto's *Four Evangelists* flanking the organ. The Molin Chapel is a pretty piece of nepotism, with a ceiling painted by Jacopo Tintoretto's son Domenico; it's upstaged, however, by a small painting of Mary with Jesus and St John by the master of roly-poly gorgeousness, Peter Paul Rubens.

◉ SANTO STEFANO
Campo Santo Stefano 3825; church free, museum €3, with Chorus pass free; ⏲ **10am-5pm Mon-Sat;** 🚊 **Accademia**
The timber ceilings of Venice's larger churches were made by boat builders, and here the *carena di nave* (ship's-keel) ceiling gives the impression that you're standing under an especially fine boat turned upside down for repairs. Duck into the side room to see two moving, brooding Tintoretto canvases: *The Last Supper,* with a ghostly little dog begging for bread, and the mostly black *Washing of the Feet.* The cloisters feature Antonio Canova's precocious 1808 funerary stelae for Giorgio Falier, showing women wrapped in cloaks and their own grief, alongside Tullio Lombardo's 1505 saint, which has such limpid, lovely upturned eyes that Titian referenced the piece for his Madonna in I Frari (p84).

VENICE >48

🛍 SHOP
🏠 ARCOBALENO *Art Supplies*
☎ **041 5236818; Calle delle Botteghe 3457;** ⏲ **9.30am-1.30pm & 3-7pm Mon-Sat;** 🚊 **Accademia**
After umpteen Venetian art masterpieces, your fingers might start twitching for a paintbrush. With shelves stocked with jars of all the essential pigments – Titian red, Tiepolo sky blue, Veronese rose, Tintoretto teal – Arcobaleno provides all the raw materials needed to start your own Venetian art movement.

🏠 ARNOLDO & BATTOIS
Handbags, Accessories
☎ **041 5285944; www.arnoldoebattois .com; Calle dei Fuseri 4271;** ⏲ **10am-1pm & 3.30-7pm Mon-Thu & Sat;** 🚊 **Sant'Angelo**
Handbags become heirlooms in the hands of designers Battois and Arnoldo, who handcraft their bags from boldly coloured leather and heraldic hardware found at Venice's antique markets. Mod yellow leather embellished with St Mark's lion door knockers create hobo bags for the arty Biennale crowd, and wide '80s belts make flashy comebacks with salamander buckles.

🏠 EBRÛ *Paper Crafts*
☎ **041 5238830; www.albertovalese -ebru.it;** ⏲ **10am-1pm & 3.30-7pm Mon-Thu & Sat;** 🚊 **Accademia**

Crazy eyes: eyeball mannequins at Fiorella Gallery

Four centuries ago, Venetian book-binders adopted the Turkish art of *ebrû*, the technique used to make marbled end-papers – but modern Venetian artisan Alberto Valese's creations are hardly by the book. His swirl-dyed silk ties may have mysterious powers to hypno-tise co-workers, while costume party masks made of psychedelic marble papier-mâché could induce Carnevale flashbacks. Inspired to make your own photo album? Ask about paper-making classes.

☐ **EPICENTRO** *Gifts, Homewares*
☎ 041 5226864; Calle dei Fabbri 932;
🕑 9.30am-1.30pm & 3-7pm Tue-Sat,
3-7pm Mon; 🚤 Vallaresso
How could you possibly survive without that Alessi soy-sauce de-

canter shaped like a hummingbird? Epicentro provides every designer household item you never knew you needed, plus the entire Alessi back catalogue of monkey-shaped sugar bowls and toothbrush-hugging trolls, all crammed into one delightful little storefront.

☐ **ESPERIENZE** *Glass, Jewellery*
☎ 041 5212945; www.esperienze venezia.com; Calle degli Specchieri 473b;
🕑 10am-noon & 3-7pm; 🚤 San Zaccharia
When Italian minimalist design meets Murano glassblowing talent and falls in love, the result is spare yet spirited glass jewellery. The creative minds behind Esperienze are a husband-and-wife team raised in Murano with a shared love of Kandinsky, Miró and other Guggenheim Collection modernist masters. Every piece is a collabora-tive effort: he literally breathes life into her designs, including blown-glass teardrop pendants and cracked-ice earrings.

☐ **FIORELLA GALLERY** *Fashion*
☎ 335 8200873; www.fiorellagallery .com; Campo Santo Stefano 2806;
🕑 3-7pm Mon, 9.30am-1.30pm & 3.30-7pm Tue-Sat; 🚤 Accademia
At Fiorella, high-heeled doge man-nequins show off subversive Vene-tian fashions hell-bent on bringing out your inner rock star. Smoking jackets are made of crushed silk

velvets in louche shades of lavender and blood red, and are then printed by hand with baroque wallpaper patterns and a Fiorella signature: wide-eyed rats. Prices start in the hundreds of euros, but check out your reflection in the graffitied Ettore Sottsass mirror and tell us you're not impressed.

🏠 GLORIA ASTOLFO *Jewellery*
☎ 041 5206827; Calle Frezzeria 1581; ⏰ 9.30am-1.30pm & 3-7pm Mon-Sat; 🚇 Vallaresso

Chandelier earrings straight out of a Venetian painting and collars of cascading pearls that would blend in with the baroque decor at La Fenice take handcrafted beadwork jewellery to the next level – but prices starting at €35 are surprisingly down to earth.

🏠 LA PIETRA FILOSOFALE
Masks
☎ 041 5285885; Calle Frezzeria 1735; ⏰ 10am-12.30pm & 3-7pm Tue-Sat; 🚇 Vallaresso

Opera stars up the road at La Fenice know La Pietra Filosofale as the go-to artisan for dramatic entrances and Carnevale costumes. Here leather is moulded by hand into fiendish scowls and deceptively innocent grins, while papier-mâché masks are sketched with expressive pen and ink patterns reminiscent of a Ca' Pesaro Klimt painting.

🏠 LE BOTTEGHE
Gifts, Sustainable Shopping
☎ 041 5227545; Ponte di Rialto 5164; ⏰ 10am-7pm Mon-Sat; 🚇 Rialto

Italian design meets global awareness at this fair-trade boutique on the steps of the Rialto. Sleek foldable straw hats made by a Bangladeshi collective in rich shades of saffron and fuchsia are just right for gondola rides, while African printed sarongs practically demand a leisurely Lido beach day.

🏠 LIBRERIA STUDIUM *Books*
☎ 041 5222382; Calle Canonica 337; ⏰ 9am-7.30pm Mon-Sat, 9.30am-1.30pm Sun; 🚇 San Zaccaria

This place has floor-to-ceiling holiday reads, including a large selection of literature in English that extends well beyond pulpy bestsellers, a section on Italian cuisine ranging from mouth-watering coffee-table books to scholarly tracts, plus a respectably vast Lonely Planet selection (not that we're biased). The book-loving staff can pluck obscure titles from high shelves for you with instant recall.

🏠 MILLEVINI *Wine*
☎ 041 5206090; Ramo del Fontego dei Turchi 5362; ⏰ 9am-1.30pm & 3.30-7pm Mon-Sat; 🚇 Rialto

This wine cave/industrial warehouse has small-producer labels and Venetian vintages, adding a touch of class amid the Rialto T-shirt kiosks and kitschy cafes. Well-versed staff help you choose and will give you the inside scoop on upcoming wine tastings.

📖 MONDADORI *Books, Music*
☎ 041 5222193; www.libreriamonda dorivenezia.it; Salizada San Moisè 1345; ⏲ 10am-7.30pm Mon-Sat, 11am-7.30pm Sun; 🚊 Vallaresso

Come for the books and music, stay for the architecture, boozing and schmoozing. The selection of CDs, mags, DVDs and novels in this Italian chain is plenty engrossing, but even precision-target shoppers will linger in the glassed-in converted cinema, which also houses Bacaro (p54), and hosts literary events and photography shows.

👓 OTTICA CARRARO *Eyeglasses*
☎ 041 5204258; www.otticacarraro.it; Calle della Mandola 3706; ⏲ 9am-1pm & 3.30-7pm Mon-Sat; 🚊 Sant'Angelo

Lost your sunglasses on the Lido? Never fear: Ottica Carraro can make you a custom pair within 24 hours. Styles range from flashy 1980s-style shades to arty matte-rubber frames that look like they were crafted from gumdrops.

👗 VENETIA STUDIUM
Fashion, Homewares
☎ 041 5236953; www.venetiastudium .com; Palazzo Zuccato, Via Larga XXII

Marzo 2425; ⏲ 10am-7pm Mon-Sat; 🚊 Santa Maria del Giglio

Get that 'just got in from Monaco for my art opening' look beloved of bohemians who marry well. The high-drama Delphos tunic dresses make anyone look like a high-maintenance modern dancer or art collector (Isadora Duncan and Peggy Guggenheim were both fans), while the hand-stamped silk-velvet bags (prices start at €50) are more arty than ostentatious.

🍴 EAT

🍴 CAFFE MANDOLA
Sandwiches €
☎ 041 5237624; Calle della Mandola 3630; ⏲ 9am-7pm Mon-Sat; 🚊 Vallaresso

Sandwiches on fresh focaccia are the speciality here: inspired fillings include tangy tuna and capers, and lean bresaola (air-dried beef), rocket and seasoned grana padano cheese. Stools provide sweet relief for tired feet if you grab your *panini* (sandwiches) outside the lunch peak and happy hour.

🍴 CAVATAPPI
Classic Venetian, Sandwiches €
☎ 041 2960252; Campo della Guerra 525-526; ⏲ 10am-8pm Tue-Thu & Sun, 10am-11pm Fri & Sat; 🚊 San Zaccaria

A stone's throw from Piazza San Marco but a world apart from

Giovanni d'Este
Sommelier and happy-hour mind-reader at I Rusteghi (p55)

Bring your compass True Venetian *osterie* [restaurant-bars] are always hidden, so you have to work a bit to get to the good stuff. **Guessing your order** Americans enjoy layered reds, like amarone; the French are used to softer wines such as ripasso, made with young valpolicella and skins from amarone. But everyone likes soave and prosecco. **Surprising Veneto wines** Pramaggiore cabernet franc is like a beautiful woman: it's very rounded and immediately gets your attention. Refosco is an ancient wine; it's in our DNA here. Our merlot is extremely elegant, with body, acidity and strength of character – it makes other merlots seem young and naive. **Anything but…** Dry spumante with cake, how horrendous! The sweetness cancels out the subtle spumante. Fragolino [strawberry-flavoured wine] is fine, but Venetians don't dunk biscuits in it. *Sgroppino* [lemon sorbet with prosecco and vodka] is ideal for cleaning your palate between courses.

overdone decor and dire tourist menus, Cavatappi is a sleek charmer with seasonal dishes, a solid selection of wines by the glass, and that rarest of San Marco finds: tasty meals that regularly come in under €15. You don't even need to look at the menu: just order the pasta or risotto of the day, ask your server to manage the wine pairing, and get the sheep's cheese drizzled with honey for dessert.

🍴 GELATOTECA SUSO
Ice Cream €
Calle della Bissa 5453; 🕑 **10am-9pm;** 🚊 **Rialto**

Ever since tabloid paparazzi captured Brangelina's brood licking Italian ice cream cones along Venetian canals, shops have popped up all over Venice promising genuine *'gelato artigianale'* – but this new hidden hotspot actually delivers handmade, local flavours. Make like a movie-star minion and upgrade to two scoops for €2.50, and don't miss the *frutti di bosco* (wild berry).

🍴 ENOTECA AL VOLTO
Cicheti, Classic Venetian €€
☎ **041 5228945; Calle Cavalli 4081;** 🕑 **10am-2pm & 5-11pm Fri-Wed;** 🚊 **Rialto**

Join the crowd working their way through the vast selection of wine and *cicheti* (Venetian tapas) at the bar, or show up early to nab a

Feel that warm glow inside at Enoteca Al Volto

table in the snug wood-beamed back room, where you'll feel like a stowaway in a ship's hold and eat like a captain. The portions of pasta with clams and white wine would satisfy even hard-working gondolieri, while thick steaks are served in a puddle of juice with a proper glass of amarone.

🍴 OSTERIA DA CARLA
Cicheti, Classic Venetian €€
☎ **041 5237855; Frezzeria 1535;** 🕑 **10am-9pm Mon-Sat;** 🚊 **Vallaresso**

While the uninitiated settle for stale pizza near Piazza San Marco, budget gourmets duck into this courtyard off Frezzeria for popularly priced pasta, wine by the glass, and crusty bread generously heaped with *baccalà mantecato* (creamy cod) and *sopressa* (soft salami). At night the kitchen gets creative, introducing grilled meats in fruit-scented reductions.

🍽 SANGAL

Inventive Venetian €€€

☎ 041 3192747; www.sangalvenice
restaurant.com; Campo San Gallo 1089;
⏰ 11.30am-3pm & 7-11pm;
🚇 Vallaresso

Warm, clever and hip without trying too hard, Sangal is everything you'd want from a Venetian date. Linger over sunsets with bubbly Veneto rosé on the terrace lounge, or settle into a banquette for piazza views and a parade of reinvented Veneto delicacies: tuna carpaccio studded with sesame and mountain herbs, succulent rabbit stuffed with handmade sausage, polenta *sformata* (savoury pudding) crisped on the outside but velvety inside, and finally, coconut-milk pannacotta enrobed in edible silver and dusted with lavender. Dinner easily tops €75 and most fusion-cuisine experiences; oenophiles, ask about wine-tasting classes.

🍽 VINI DA ARTURO *Steak* €€€

☎ 041 5286974; Calle degli Assassini 3656;
⏰ 7-11pm Mon-Sat; 🚇 Sant'Angelo

You could flirt with the pasta menu, but everyone in this cor-ridor-sized eight-table restaurant comes for the same reason: the steak. Studded with green peppercorns, soused in brandy and mustard, or rare on the bone, these thick, tender slabs could be cut with a butter knife. *And* they deserve Hollywood credits – your host will happily trot out irrefutable proof that Nicole Kidman actually eats and that director Joel Silver managed to escape *The Matrix* for dinner here.

🍸 DRINK

🍸 B BAR *Lounge*

☎ 041 2406819; www.bauervenezia
.com; Campo San Moisè 1459; ⏰ 6pm-
1am Wed-Sun; 🚇 San Marco, Vallaresso

Pose as glitterati at your booth in the gold-mosaic B Bar, where top-shelf cocktails are thoughtfully served with bar nibbles and the piano player plays softly so as not to upstage VIP guests such as yourself. There's an entire menu of creative twists on the classic Venetian *spritz* (prosecco-based cocktail), including the bittersweet Rialto, with prosecco, gin and a splash of grenadine.

🍸 BACARO *Lounge*

☎ 041 2960687; Salizada San Moisè 1348;
⏰ 9am-2am; 🚇 San Marco, Vallaresso

Bacaro has good looks and smarts too: the bar is a shimmering mosaic oval that reflects well on you, and the company you'll keep is terribly clever, especially once the crowd moves here after literary events at Mondadori (p51), next door.

▶ HARRY'S BAR *Lounge*
☎ 041 5285777; Calle Vallaresso 1323; ⏱ noon-11pm; 🚉 San Marco, Vallaresso

Since almost every major 20th-century American talent has imbibed here – Charlie Chaplin, Ernest Hemingway, Truman Capote, Orson Welles – there's a theory that genius is stirred into these cocktails. Yes, the €18 peach-and-prosecco Bellini is named after the Venetian painter of Madonnas with peachy complexions, and best imbibed at the bar where it was invented. Since Harry's menu is among the most high-end in Venice, you might expect a gilded risotto. But the surprise is how down to earth the whole operation is, with simple bistro chairs, small tables set close together, and straightforward service with zero affectation. Harry's Bar is now an empire, with locations in London and Hong Kong, and packaged pasta sold under the Cipriani label, but there's no substitute for the original.

▶ I RUSTEGHI *Wine Bar*
☎ 041 5232205; Corte del Tentor 5513; ⏱ 10.30am-3pm & 6-9.30pm Mon-Sat; 🚉 Rialto

A *giro d'ombra* (pub crawl) becomes a gourmet journey of discovery with fourth-generation sommelier and owner Giovanni d'Este (p52), who'll open exceptional vintages for you to sample by the glass with artisanal cheeses, boar salami and velvety *lardo di Colonnata* (cured pork fat). Ask Giovanni to choose your wine, and he'll give you a long look to assess your character before presenting you with his selection – high compliments being a big-hearted Refosco or starry-eyed Vermentino.

▶ TEAMO *Tearoom, Bar*
☎ 347 3665016; Rio Terà della Mandola 3795; ⏱ 9am-10pm; 🚉 Sant'Angelo

When the sun sets, Piazza San Marco scenesters disappear like packs of premature Cinderellas – only to reappear moments later at Teamo, lured by a vast *cicheti* spread atop the glowing alabaster bar, €3.50 Tocai friulano white wine, and a hip, gay-friendly scene.

▶ TORINO@NOTTE
Cafe-Bar
☎ 041 5223914; Campo San Luca 4592; ⏱ 8pm-1am Tue-Sat; 🚉 Rialto

Freeform, eclectic and loud, Torino adds an element of the unexpected to postdinner drinks in otherwise staid San Marco. On any given night you can enjoy a €2 to €4 drink with music provided by a live band, a spontaneous college-student singalong or a collection of scratchy reggae records played by a friend of the bartender.

⭐ PLAY

⭐ CAFFÈ FLORIAN
Classical Music, Jazz

☎ 041 5205641; Piazza San Marco 56-59; ⏰ 10am-11pm Tue-Thu; 🚶 San Marco, Vallaresso

Tango, anyone? Without the daily accompaniment of the Caffè Florian house orchestra, the sun might not be allowed to set in Venice. Florian mostly sticks to rituals established in 1720 – unctuously charming uniformed waiters, gooey hot chocolate served on a silver tray, lovers canoodling on plush banquettes indoors – but has updated its musical repertoire to about 1950 to include jazz and Latin numbers. Since that hot chocolate will cost you €10 (with a €6 surcharge for piazza seating), you may as well stick around for the sunset grand finale, when the fading light illuminates the Basilica di San Marco's portal mosaics. The Florian encourages impromptu piazza dance performances with DOC wines by the glass, served alongside complimentary olives and crisps – all for less than a San Marco cappuccino.

⭐ CENTRALE *DJs, Live Music*
☎ 041 2960664; www.centrale-lounge.com; Piscina Frezzeria 1659b; ⏰ 6.30pm-2am Wed-Mon; 🚶 San Marco, Vallaresso

The optional bodyguard service may seem a bit much but, with its nocturnal instincts and low-key cool, Centrale is Venice's VIP magnet. Within these exposed-brick walls you might spot Juliette Binoche, Spike Lee and sundry Italian moguls, all moodily lit by Murano chandeliers. Meal prices are high, but Centrale draws late-night crowds for drinks, snacks, chill-out DJ sets and occasional live music.

⭐ INTERPRETI VENEZIANI
Classical Music

☎ 041 2770561; www.interpreti veneziani.com; Chiesa San Vidal, Campo San Vidal 2862b; adult/student & senior €25/20; ⏰ from 8.30pm; 🚶 Accademia

Everything you knew of Vivaldi from phone ring-tones is proved fantastically wrong. Interpreti Veneziani play Vivaldi as a soundtrack for this city of intrigue: you'll never listen to *The Four Seasons* again without hearing summer storms gathering over the lagoon and steps echoing over footbridges in a winter's night intrigue. Three members of the talented Amadio family (p129) are among the featured soloists, who pull startling vibrations from original

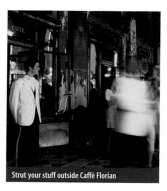
Strut your stuff outside Caffè Florian

18th-century instruments and upstage San Vidal's vivid Carpaccio altarpiece.

⭐ MUSICA A PALAZZO *Opera*
☎ 340 9717272; www.musicapalazzo.com; Palazzo Barbarigo-Minotto, Fondamenta Duodo o Barbarigo 2504; ticket €50; ⏱ doors open 8pm; ⚓ Santa Maria del Giglio

In these intimate settings, the soprano's high notes might make you fear for your wineglass, and the thundering baritone is felt in the base of your spine. The 1½-hour show feels more like a decadent baroque party than a performance, with 70 guests – wineglasses in tow – following opera singers and orchestra from receiving room to salon to private quarters. The singers are in modern dress, but instead of appearing theatrical or anachronistic, they seem to be pouring their hearts out, pleading their cases with Verdi and drawing you into their Rossini intrigues.

⭐ TEATRO LA FENICE
Classical Music, Opera
☎ tickets 041 2424, theatre 041 786511; www.teatrolafenice.it; Campo San Fantin 1965; ticket price varies; ⏱ varies; ⚓ Santa Maria del Giglio

International opera reputations are still made and lost on this postage stamp of a stage, just as they have been for centuries, despite two fires and countless backstage intrigues. La Fenice (the Phoenix) has risen from the ashes of a 1996 arson, and the grand new theatre remains true to the baroque blueprints of 1836. The stage is encircled by box seating dripping with gold and decorated with sweet-faced babies rather precociously weaving garlands and playing musical instruments. **Tours** (☎ 041 2424; adult/student €7/5) are possible with advance booking by phone, but the best way to see La Fenice is with the *loggione*, opera buffs that pass judgment on productions from on high in the top-tier cheap seats. In between performances and in the opera off season, symphonies and chamber-music concerts are irresistible draws at La Fenice.

>CASTELLO

Sailors, saints and modern artists have made Castello what it is today: a waterfront home to earthy *osterie* (restaurant-bars), ethereal icons and the show-stopper that is the Biennale. Churches are gilt to the hilt, historic four-star hotels sprawl along the Grand Canal waterfront, and the Biennale pavilions are showpieces of modern architecture. Venice's Armenian and Greek communities once lived in these winding lanes alongside Turkish and Syrian merchants, bringing to the neighbourhood a cosmopolitan flair that's still noticeable in local restaurants, as well as even more glittering icons. But Castello has proven that it's possible to be refined in the extreme without losing that vital roughness around the edges: some 5000 shipbuilders once worked here in the Arsenale, building the fleet that extended Venice's empire to Constantinople. Traces of those glory days can be found in the Museo Storico Navale and in the odd bawdy joke at happy hour.

CASTELLO

👁 SEE

👁 BIENNALE PAVILIONS

www.labiennale.org; 👤 Giardini
In between Art Biennales (in odd-numbered years), the public gardens here are for lovers, who stroll aimlessly amid landmarks of modern architecture. Gothically romantic vines creep up to cover the Palladian-style British Pavilion, and picnickers canoodle between the mosaic-detailed secessionist-style Austro-Hungarian Pavilion and the disappointingly derivative US Pavilion. Pavilions cover just about every major modernist movement and construction material, from the '70s ski-lodge stylings of the timber Canadian building to the metal-clad Korean Pavilion in a converted electrical plant. James Stirling's 1991 Book Pavilion is more interesting from the inside, Italy's blindingly white Fascist-era pavilion is grandiose and Peter Cox's 1988 Australian Pavilion (intended to be temporary) looks like a mobile home – but it's hard to compete with the hometown favourite Carlo Scarpa's clever raw-concrete-and-glass Venezuelan Pavilion from 1954, which still looks avant-garde. See p17 and p29 for more on the Biennale.

👁 FONDAZIONE QUERINI STAMPALIA

☎ 041 2711411; www.querinistampalia.it; Ponte Querini 5252; adult/student €10/8; ⏱ 10am-7pm Tue-Sun; 👤 San Zaccaria
Modern meets baroque in this 16th-century *palazzo* (palace or mansion), which was updated by Carlo Scarpa in the 1940s, and had a Mario Botta–designed cafe and bookshop added in the1990s. The middle floors preserve the graces of bygone centuries, with porcelain displays on silk-clad walls and an entire Giovanni Bellini room; downstairs, Scarpa's Islamic-inspired water channels run through the ground floor and into the courtyard fountain. Top-floor modern-art shows are hit-and-miss, but major draws include the fanciful Jacopo Guarana-frescoed master bedroom, leisurely lunches in Scarpa's garden and Saturday concerts in the baroque music room.

👁 MUSEO DELLE ICONE

☎ 041 5226581; www.istitutoellenico.org; Campiello dei Greci 3412; adult/student €4/2; ⏱ 9am-5pm; 👤 San Zaccaria
Glowing colours and all-seeing eyes fill the gallery of the Museum of Icons, a treasure trove of elegant Greek icons made in 14th- to 17th-century Italy. Especially impressive is the expressive *San Giovanni Climaco*, which shows the saintly author of a Greek spiritual guide distracted from his

E **F** **G** **H**

1

Bacini di
Carenaggio

2

Darsena
Grande

● Arsenale
  Nuovo

San
Pietro

3

Rio delle Vergini

Ponte
San Daniele

C Larga
San Pietro

Campo
San
Pietro

Cattedrale
di San Pietro
di Castello

LA TANA

Arsenale

Campo
di Auga

Isola de
San Pietro

Fond della Tana

Corte Nuova

Corte del
Bianco

Campiello
d'Pomeri

a Giuseppe Garibaldi

Fond di Sant'Anna

Rio di Quintavalle

4

Riva dei Sette Martiri

Viale Garibaldi

C Stretta Sarestn

San Domenico

C delle Ancore

C Correra

Canale di San Pietro

Sero Marina

Fond San Giuseppe

Giardini

Viale Trento

Giardini
Pubblici

Rio Terà San Giuseppe
Paludo di S.Antonio

SANT'ELENA

Darsena di
Sant'Elena

5

Viale Theatre

25

Biennale

Rio de Partigiani

1

Viale Quattro Novembre

Campo del
Grappa

Isola di
Sant'Elena

6

Parco delle
Rimembranze

C Gen.Chinotto

Rio del Quarent

work by visions of souls diving into hell. The building itself is a monument to the city's religious tolerance: this seat of Venice's Greek Orthodox community was built by Baldassare Longhena, Venice's official architect, and served as a hospital for the poor into the 20th century.

⬤ MUSEO STORICO NAVALE

☎ 041 5200276; www.marina.difesa.it; Fondamenta dell'Arsenale 2148; admission €1.55; ⏰ 8.45am-1.30pm Mon-Fri, 8.45am-1pm Sat; 🚇 Arsenale

The improbable tale of Venice's seafaring empire (see p166) and the city's lingering fascination with boats unfolds in rambling fashion across four floors and 42 rooms of painstakingly detailed boat models and fearsome weaponry – which was rarely used within Venice, but was kept on hand at the Arsenale, just in case. The fanciest boat is the model of the *bucintoro* (ducal barge), used in ceremonial occasions such as the Sposalizio del Mar (Wedding to the Sea; see p28). But Peggy Guggenheim's gondola isn't shabby either, and the ocean liners and WWII battleships are fascinating.

Pimp my *bucintoro* (ducal barge)? Check out the the dogi's gilt-y pleasures at the Museo Storico Navale

THE ORPHAN ORCHESTRAS OF VENICE

Music was the salvation of orphans in Venice, and orphans came to the city's rescue. Sounds like something out of Dickens, but it's true.

In the 16th to 18th centuries, circumstances conspired to produce an unprecedented number of Venetian orphans: on the one hand was the plague and snake-oil cures, which decimated the adult population; on the other was flourishing prostitution, scandalous masquerade parties at island nunneries, and the fashion among Venetian ladies to take a *cicisbeo* (young manservant) while their husbands were at sea. The state took on the care and musical training of the city's orphan girls, who in turn earned their keep in orchestras and choirs that performed at balls and public functions. Venice's glitterati turned out for these early black-tie fundraisers, with musical performances directed by such maestri as Domenico Cimarosa and Vivaldi, who found steady employment for decades composing for orphan-girl orchestras. Visiting dignitaries treated to orphan concerts were well advised to tip the performers: you never knew whose illegitimate daughter you might be insulting otherwise.

Venice's latest attraction came not a moment too soon, as it helped establish Venice as the leisure-class capital of Europe just as its trade economy was failing. Orphans no longer dominate Venetian orchestras, but you can still hear the baroque music they popularised; for details, see p159.

🅖 PALAZZO GRIMANI

☎ 041 5200345; www.palazzogrimani
.org; Ramo Grimani 4858; guided tours
adult/student & senior €9/5, with Gallerie dell'Accademia admission €14/7.50;
🕓 tours 10am, noon & 3pm Tue-Sun;
🚊 San Zaccaria

After 27 years of restoration, the 16th-century frescoed splendours of this Renaissance palace are revealed. Predatory birds circle over trompe-l'oeil salon forests; snickering grotesques upstage mythological heroes in the dining room; and a stairway cameo depicts elderly Doge Grimani receiving Justice, 40 years after his Inquisition trial for humanist heresy.

🅖 SAN FRANCESCO DELLA VIGNA

☎ 041 5206102; Campo San Francesco
della Vigna 2787; 🕓 8.30am-12.30pm &
3-7pm; 🚊 Celestia

Don't be fooled by its inconspicuous location: this enchanting Franciscan church is an all-star Venetian art showcase. Designed by Jacopo Sansovino, it was graced with a classical facade by a young Palladio, and father-and-son sculptors Pietro and Tullio Lombardo sheathed Cappella Giustiniani with marble reliefs as expressive as cartoons. Inside, the church positively glows with Bellini's beatific *Madonna and Saints* and Antonio da Negroponte's delightful *Virgin*

Gothic Zanipolo (pictured on right)

Enthroned, with angels swimming and birds strutting around an utterly unfazed Madonna.

◎ SAN ZACCARIA

☎ 041 5221257; Campo San Zaccaria 4693; Cappella di Sant'Anastasia €1; 🕑 10am-noon & 4-6pm Mon-Sat, 4-6pm Sun; 🚊 San Zaccaria

If these walls could talk, they'd tell tales of a former life as a convent for the daughters of Venice's upper crust, who passed their time here in prayer, concerts and rather scandalous masked balls. The influence of this church is visible in its wealth of art: a 12th-century Roman-Byzantine mosaic floor, the dazzling gilt polyptych in the Golden Chapel, Bellini's melancholy enthroned Madonna, and Giambattista Tiepolo's version of the flight into Egypt in a Venetian boat. Don't miss Antonio Vivarini's 1443

painting of St Sabina, who keeps her cool as angels buzz around her head like lagoon mosquitoes.

◎ ZANIPOLO

Basilica dei Santi Giovanni e Paolo; ☎ 041 5235913; Campo Santi Giovanni e Paolo 6363; admission €2.50; 🕑 9.30am-6pm Mon-Sat, 1-6pm Sun; 🚊 Ospedale

This Gothic church is big enough to house several masterpieces, 25 tombs of dogi (Venice's leaders) by such notable artists as Nicolo Pisano and Tullio Lombardo, and examples of most major architectural styles to hit Venice since work began on the church in 1333. The first chapel on the right holds Giambattista Lorenzetti's baroque relief of *Jesus the Navigator,* with Jesus looking at the moon and searching the stars like a Venetian sea captain. Another wonderful work is Guido Reni's *San Giuseppe,* showing Joseph exchanging tender, adoring looks with baby Jesus. Since the church is connected to Venice's main hospital, the Ospedale Civile, one of the most popular shrines is the one to Venetian James Salomoni, patron of cancer patients, whose own wounds are said to have emitted a 'heavenly fragrance' after his death. But the most popular piece is Paolo Veronese's ceiling depicting the rosy Virgin being crowned by cherubs as she ascends a staircase, with angels flipping with the joy of it all.

🏠 SHOP

🏠 ARTE VETRO MURANO *Glass*
☎ 041 5237514; www.artevetromurano
.com; Calle della Rasse 4613; ⏱ 10am-
1pm & 3-6pm Mon-Sat; 🚶 San Zaccaria

Shatter glass conventions with new styles by emerging Murano glass designers: Davide Penso makes a necklace of flat puddles of orange glass that have a molten-lava look about them, while Artematte's deliberately mismatched lampwork glass earrings will earn you double takes at Biennale art openings.

🏠 BANCO 10
Fashion, Sustainable Shopping
☎ 041 5221439; Salizada Sant'Antonin 3478a; ⏱ 10am-1pm & 3.30-7pm Tue-Sat; 🚶 San Zaccaria

Prison orange is so over. All the swirly skirts, sleek jackets, tapestry handbags and diva dresses in this nonprofit boutique are made as part of a retraining program at the women's prison on Giudecca, funding their continuing career training and reintegration into society after release. Sumptuous silks, velvets and tapestry are donated by Fortuny and Bevilacqua, designs are created by female inmates, and volunteers sell them in this truly inspired boutique. Even La Fenice has dressed its divas in costumes made through the program.

🏠 BARBIERI ARABESQUE
Scarves & Ties
☎ 041 5228177; Ponte dei Greci 3403; ⏱ 10am-7.30pm; 🚶 San Zaccaria

La Fenice nights call for Como silk stoles and cravats, while sunset gondola rides require whisper-light wool shawls and dapper ascots – luckily, Barbieri has you and your neck stylishly covered. Look for store-label pop art ties and Mediterranean blue ombre beach wraps at outlet-store prices.

🏠 GIOVANNA ZANELLA *Shoes*
☎ 041 5235500; Calle Carminati 5641; ⏱ 9.30am-1pm & 3-7pm Mon-Sat; 🚶 Rialto

Woven, sculpted, and crested like birds, Zanella's shoes practically demand a red carpet. The Venetian designer custom-makes the shoes, so the answer is always, 'Yes, you can get those peep-toe numbers in yellow and grey, size 12, extra narrow.' It'll cost you of course, but at least you won't be upstaged by Angelina Jolie in the same pair at the Venice Film Festival.

🏠 PAROLE E MUSICA *Music*
☎ 041 5235010; www.intermusic.biz; Salizada San Lio 5673; ⏱ 10am-7.30pm Mon-Sat, 11am-7.30pm Sun; 🚶 Rialto

Head to this store to take Venice's music home with you. Specialising in Italian pop, classical and opera, it has new Italian recordings and

European indie labels that are hard to find elsewhere.

☐ SCHEGGE *Masks*
☎ 041 5225789; Calle Lunga Santa Maria Formosa 6185; ☾ 10am-9pm Mon-Sat; ☖ Rialto

Go incognito in style with this shop's highly original masks, which are inspired by influences as diverse as Gothic architecture and the paintings of Amedeo Modigliani. Well into the night, you'll find this mother-daughter team wielding tiny paintbrushes, coaxing minute baroque tendrils into bloom along the side of a mask.

☐ SIGFRIDO CIPOLATO
Jewellery
☎ 041 5228437; San Lio Caselleria 5336; ☾ 10am-1pm & 3-7pm Mon-Sat; ☖ San Zaccaria

A dazzling Carnevale mask

The window display here looks like a baroque jewel box: chandelier earrings ending in tiny gold skulls, Fabergé-incised enamel rings with emeralds, free-form pearls set in diamonds. Though they may look like heirlooms, these small wonders were created by Sigfrido (p116), who uses techniques handed down through generations.

⫟ EAT
⫟ AL COVO
Inventive Venetian €€€
☎ 041 5223812; www.ristorantealcovo .com; Campiello della Pescaria 3968; ☾ 12.45-3.30pm & 7.30pm-midnight Fri-Tue; ☖ Arsenale

This place has all the makings of a classic Venetian *osteria* – low-beamed ceilings, exposed brick wall, regulars in the corner – but its typical dishes come with a twist. Caprese salad gets the Covo treatment, with basil and *mozzarella di bufala* (buffalo mozzarella) served with a heavenly cherry-tomato jelly; squid-ink pasta comes with clams and zucchini flowers; and Adriatic tuna is accompanied by five sauces. Top-quality seafood and produce carefully sourced from around the lagoon explain the somewhat stiff à la carte prices, offset by well-priced boutique wines available per full or half bottle. The best investment is the free-form three-course dinner, which gives you your pick of starter or pasta, plus a main and dessert or cheese plate for €52.

AL PORTEGO
Cicheti, Classic Venetian €

☎ 041 5229038; Calle della Malvasia 6015; ⏱ 10.30am-3pm & 6-10pm Mon-Sat; 🚇 Rialto

Marco Polo may have had an easier time finding China than you'll have locating this *osteria* hunkered under an archway – but for *cicheti* beyond the usual *panini,* it's quite a find. Come early to grab a stool and the last order of pasta with plump scampi, or join the bar crowd enjoying *frittura mista* (fried seafood) and *seppia in nero* (squid in its own ink) with polenta. Wines are cheekily listed next to a vintage poster listing Venetian bordello rates (soap cost extra).

CONCA D'ORO *Pizza* €€

☎ 041 5229293; Campo Santi Filippo e Giacomo 4338; ⏱ noon-3.30pm & 6.30-10.30pm; 🚇 San Zaccaria

Pizza is not a local speciality – in case you hadn't guessed from the cardboard pies you'll find at eateries pandering to the tourist trade around San Marco – but this place is the exception. This local joint right behind San Marco brought pizza to Venice in 1960, and has been slinging generous thin-crust pies with creative toppings ever since. It's not especially quick

about it, though, so relax and enjoy the sun in the piazza and the Italian ska blaring on the stereo.

IL RIDOTTO
Inventive Venetian €€€

☎ 041 5208280; www.ilridotto.com; Campo Santi Filippo e Giacomo 4509; ⏱ 7-11pm Thu, noon-3pm & 7-11pm Fri-Tue; 🚇 San Zaccaria

From an open kitchen the size of a closet comes a parade of tasty small plates: a dollop of savoury Tuscan bread pudding, Venetian seafood composed into a glistening mosaic, a silky *panna cotta*. Mains are less satisfying and quite pricey, so you might want to stick to an assortment of antipasti and *primi*. There are only five close-set tables (10 seats total), and your dishes are delivered on Versace china by chef/owner Gianni Bonacorsi himself. Ask for pairing advice: Gianni's restaurant is snug and modern, but his cellar is vast and historic.

TAVERNA SAN LIO
Inventive Venetian €€

☎ 041 2770669; www.tavernasanlio.com; Salizada San Lio 5547; ⏱ 7-11pm Tue-Sat; 🚇 Rialto

Modern without losing Venice's essential quirkiness, this place handles its seafood dishes delicately: go with the seasonal choice of scallops with thyme, pink pepper and saffron, or with homemade

Wine and pizza: the perfect Italian lunch

sea bream ravioli with a mint-pesto sauce, paired with the sprightly house pinot grigio. Low wood tables encourage diners to lean towards one another conspiratorially, amoeba-shaped lamps set the mood for free-form conversation and huge windows let you in on the catwalk action outdoors.

TRATTORIA CORTE SCONTA
Inventive Venetian €€€
☎ 041 5227024; Calle del Pestrin 3886; 🕙 11.30am-3.30pm & 6-10.30pm Tue-Sat; 🚇 Arsenale
Artistry meets cuisine in this garden retreat between the Biennale and Rialto. Chef Eugenio Oro celebrates Venice's lagoon locale with creative cuisine that combines seasonal seafood with Rialto market finds: buttery

bream with tangy redcurrants and arugula, or squid-ink pasta topped by zucchini flowers, scallops and a chiffonade of island herbs. Oro single-handedly revives traditional dishes like *uove di seppie* (squid eggs), which must be gingerly removed without rupturing the ink sac and lightly poached to retain their delicate, un-fishy flavour. Don't miss the seafood appetiser, with glistening crustaceans arranged like paint dabs on a Venetian artist's palette.

ZENZERO *Cicheti, Pastries* €
☎ 041 2412828; Campo Santa Marina 5902; 🕙 9am-8pm Mon-Sat; 🚇 Rialto
As you might guess from the dapper chef-owners behind the counter in their colour-coordinated jumpers, every order here comes with extra helpings of flair: homemade croissants have nutty *grana padano* cheese baked right into the crust, puff pastry comes crowned with puréed truffle, Treviso rocket salads are drizzled with aged balsamic, wines are DOC quality and impeccable cappuccino is served with a star-shaped cocoa stencil.

Y DRINK
Y BAR TERAZZA DANIELI
Rooftop Lounge
☎ 041 5226480; www.starwoodhotels .com; Riva degli Schiavoni 4196; 🕙 3.30-6.30pm May-Sep; 🚇 San Zaccaria

Watch San Giorgio Maggiore blush in the late-afternoon sun over drinks at the most romantic rooftop bar in Venice – preferably the signature Danieli cocktail of gin, apricot and orange juices with a splash of grenadine. Besides canal views and rooftop breezes, double-digit drinks come with complimentary snacks and the occasional celebrity sighting.

�my NOTECA MASCARETA
Wine Bar
☎ 041 5230744; Calle Lunga Santa Maria Formosa 5183; ⏳ **7pm-2am Fri-Tue;** 🚤 **San Zaccaria**
Generous appetiser platters of local cured meats and artisan cheeses could pass for a meal, and your host Mauro can hardly be stopped from pouring you his choice of 100 wines for €2 to €4 a glass. In good weather, the outdoor bar is the place to feast on *cicheti* and an *ombra* (glass) of organic wine for under €10.

☧ PARADISO *Cafe-Bar*
☎ 335 6223079; Giardini Pubblici 1260; ⏳ **9am-7pm;** 🚤 **Biennale**
At Paradiso, curators woo shy artists on mod couches and star architects hold court under sun umbrellas, even between Biennales. The scene is fuelled by a steady stream of coffee and cocktails that cost less than you'd expect given the designer

chairs, waterfront location and lack of competition – this is the only cafe within reach of anyone in stilettos at the Biennale.

☧ TAVERNA L'OLANDESE VOLANTE *Pub*
☎ 041 5289349; Salizada San Lio 5658; ⏳ **10am-2pm & 5pm-12.30am Mon-Sat, 10am-2pm Sun;** 🚤 **Rialto**
Chaos reigns at the Flying Dutchman, where study-abroad students mingle easily and laugh loudly with local eccentrics over cheap beer. On summer nights, expect to go home happily hoarse.

★ PLAY
▣ COLLEGIUM DUCALE
Classical Music
☎ 041 984252; www.collegiumducale.com; Palazzo delle Prigioni; adult/student & senior €25/20; ⏳ **show 9pm;** 🚤 **San Zaccaria**
Spend a perfectly enjoyable evening in prison with a seven-member chamber orchestra, whose grace notes of Albinoni, Bach and Corelli escape the high, barred windows of a converted cell that once held Venice's political prisoners. Opera divas occasionally perform with piano accompaniment, and arias can get loud in this reverberating stone hall – but the vaulted ceilings carry haunting low notes that would be lost in an open-air concert venue.

>CANNAREGIO

Anyone could adore Venice on looks alone, but in Cannaregio you'll fall for its personality. Located between extroverted San Marco and introverted Santa Croce, earthy Castello and saintly San Polo, Cannaregio combines all of its neighbours' personality quirks. Day trippers race along broad Strada Nova en route from the train to the Rialto, while just a few streets over, footsteps echo along moody stretches of Fondamenta della Misericordia without a T-shirt kiosk in sight. The Jewish Ghetto (p19) is a tribute to the tough, tolerant community of Cannaregio, who stuck it out on these malarial swamps; both top-floor synagogues and Gothic churches are integral parts of the scenery. At night, students from nearby Ca' Foscari University and visitors who are loath to leave converge on local *osterie* (restaurant-bars) for drinks, gossip and some of Venice's least-known and best-priced dinners.

CANNAREGIO

◎ SEE

🛍 SHOP

🍴 EAT

🍸 DRINK

⭐ PLAY

Please see over for map

◉ SEE

◉ CA' D'ORO

☎ 041 5200345; www.cadoro.org;
Calle di Ca' d'Oro 3932; adult/EU student
under 26yr/EU under 18yr & over 65yr
€6.50/3.25/free; ⏲ 8.15am-2pm Mon,
8.15am-7.15pm Tue-Sun; 🚢 Ca' d'Oro

Napoleon had excellent taste in plunder, as this palace museum reveals. Until Baron Franchetti donated Ca' d'Oro to Venice as an art museum (along with his personal art collection), the paintings, reliefs and sculpture taken from Veneto churches during Napoleon's Italy conquest were warehoused at Milan's Brera museum. Highlights include Andrea Mantegna's magnificent altarpiece of a teeth-baring, blood-dripping, arrow-riddled *St Sebastian;* Pietro Lombardo's tender *Madonna and Child* in glistening Carrara marble; and a faded but still sensuous nude on a fragment of a fresco by Giorgione. The palace itself is a masterwork of *palazzo* (palace or mansion) architecture, with its Gothic Grand Canal balcony and marble-mosaic ground floor, even though it was long ago stripped of the polychrome marble and gold leaf cladding that gave it its name (House of Gold).

◉ CAMPO DEL GHETTO NUOVO

www.ghetto.it; 🚢 San Marcuola

Look around: this lopsided plaza that serves as a community playground was once the unofficial centre of Venice's shipping empire. Jews were originally only allowed to live in Giudecca, but Venice saw the benefit in keeping its bankers, textile merchants and artisans close at hand, and in 1385 allowed Armenian, Jewish, Turkish and Greek communities to reside in Venice proper. Hundreds of Spanish Jews found refuge from the Inquisition here in 1589, but a plaque on the wall recalls the dark days of 5 December 1943 and 17 August 1944, when Venetian Jews were sent to Fossoli concentration camp; 289 were deported to Nazi death camps. The Jewish retirement home along the northeast side of the square once housed survivors. Legend has it that a ghostly rabbi

Campo del Ghetto Nuovo

who was spotted in various locations around the square after the WWII deportations mysteriously reappeared in the 1990s. See p19 for more about the Ghetto.

CHIESA DELLA MADONNA DELL'ORTO

☎ 041 2750462; Campo della Madonna dell'Orto 3520; adult/under 10yr €3/free, with Chorus pass free; ☀ 10am-5pm Mon-Sat; ☗ Madonna dell'Orto

One of Venice's best-kept secrets is this elegantly spare brick Gothic cathedral dedicated to ferrymen, merchants and travellers (hey, that's you), which was the object of Tintoretto's attention (see p15) for decades. No wonder: he lived just over the footbridge from here. Offsetting his stormy *Last Judgment* masterpiece in the apse is his golden-tinged *Presentation of the Virgin in the Temple*, where an assembly of angels, saints and mere mortals crane their necks to watch her ascend these staggering heights, pointing her out as a shining example to their children. Tintoretto and his family are buried in the corner chapel.

CHIESA DI SANTA MARIA DEI MIRACOLI

☎ 041 715359; Campo dei Miracoli 6074; adult/under 10yr €3/free, with Chorus pass free; ☀ 10am-5pm Mon-Sat; ☗ Rialto

When Nicolò di Pietro's Madonna icon started miraculously weeping in its outdoor shrine in 1480, crowd control became impossible in this cramped corner of Cannaregio. Out of deference to her holiness – and possibly to disperse foot-traffic jams – the neighbours took up a collection to build a chapel to house the painting and its ecstatic admirers. But there was another miracle in store for the neighbourhood: the church itself. In his design, Pietro Lombardo completely ignored the then popular Gothic style in favour of a simpler, more classical approach that would come to be known as Renaissance architecture. This jewel box of a church is clad inside and out with glistening marble and, in a prime example of Renaissance humanism, Pier Maria Pennacchi filled each of the 50 wooden ceiling panels with a bright-eyed portrait of a saint or prophet dressed as a Venetian. What started as a modest chapel became a monument to community, and a true icon of Venetian ingenuity.

MUSEO EBRAICO DI VENEZIA

☎ 041 715359; www.museoebraico.it; Campo del Ghetto Nuovo 2902b; adult/student €3/2, ind synagogues tour €8.50/7; ☀ 10am-7pm Sun-Fri Jun-Sep, 10am-6pm Sun-Fri Oct-May; ☗ San Marcuola

More than a collection of Jewish artefacts, the Museo Ebraico di Venezia is a starting point for exploring this vibrant Venetian community and its pivotal roles in Venetian arts, architecture, commerce and history. English-language tours take you inside three to four of the seven tiny synagogues in the Ghetto, and leave every hour starting at 10.30am. Guided English-language tours of the recently restored Antico Cimitero Israelitico (Ancient Jewish Cemetery; p134) are also available on Sundays by prior reservation with the museum. See p19 for more about Venice's Jewish community.

🛍 SHOP
🛍 GIANNI BASSO STAMPATORE *Paper Crafts*
☎ 041 5234681; Calle del Fumo 5306; ⏰ 9am-1pm & 2-6pm Mon-Fri, 9am-1pm Sat; 🚊 Fondamente Nuove

The window display of business cards printed here demonstrates Signor Basso's typesetting prowess: restaurant critic Gael Greene's features a knife and fork, conductor Michael Tilson Thomas' title rises from a grand piano, and Hugh Grant's moniker appears alongside a remarkably tame lion. Choose your own insignia, drawn from Gianni's collection of antique illustrated books.

📖 SOLARIS *Books*
☎ 041 5241098; www.libreriasolaris.com; Rio Terà della Maddelena 2332; ⏰ 10.15am-12.30pm & 2.30-7pm Mon-Sat, 10.30am-12.30pm & 4-7pm Sun; 🚊 San Marcuola

The plot thickens at Venice's landmark bookstore for comics, mysteries and science fiction. The tiny store is packed with DVDs, books and periodicals, with a back wall that's a big curved bookcase. There's an entire section for *Corto Maltese,* the graphic novels by comics master Hugo Pratt, the most famous of which are set in Venice.

🍴 EAT
🍴 AL CICHETI *Cicheti*   €
☎ 041 716037; Calle della Misericordia 367; ⏰ 7.30am-7.30pm Mon-Fri, 7.30am-1pm Sat; 🚊 Ferrovia

Train or plane food would be a terrible way to end your stay in Venice, so stop by this *bacaro* (bar) near the station to toast your trip with a glass of prosecco and a plate of *pasta e ceci* (pasta with chickpeas).

🍴 AL FONTEGO DEI PESCATORI
Inventive Venetian   €€€
☎ 041 5200538; Calle Priuli 3726; ⏰ noon-3pm & 7-10.30pm Tue-Sun; 🚊 Rialto

Just when you think you know Venetian seafood and speciality

Rosanna Corró
Paper artisan and designer of book-bound handbags at Carté (p87)

Cosmopolitan paper I started out as a book restorer, and I had access to private collections of ancient books with incredible marbled end papers. The tradition of *carta marmorizzata* [marbled paper] was brought to Venice from Japan via Turkey and Florence, and it evolved every step of the way. When I studied these ancient methods, I saw new possibilities too, things I could bring to the tradition as a Brazilian and Venetian with a modern sensibility.

Cannaregio calm There's design inspiration right at my doorstep: ancient walls with peeling plaster, the reflection of light on the water, Madonna dell'Orto [p74]. The ratio is about five Venetians for every three tourists, and it's peaceful and sunny along the *fondamente* [canal banks]. **Capturing Venice's mood** No two sheets turn out the same, because each depends on the temperature of the water, the humidity, the mood of that day. If I can capture that moment on paper, I'm happy.

produce, this creative garden restaurant cheerfully proves you wrong. Start with Orlogio (Clock), with polenta triangles pointing to 12 types of lagoon seafood, or Poker, where seafood comes raw and flavours are wild – think squid with balsamic blackberries and bass with *alchechenge* (ground cherry). Chase with a lava-tinged Veneto Lugana white, and follow with seasonal gnocchi or pasta, invented daily – as host Lollo jokes, 'it's tested on friends, not on animals'.

☷ ALLA VEDOVA
Cicheti, Classic Venetian €

☎ 041 5285324; Calle del Pistor 3912; ⏱ 11.30am-2pm & 6.30-10.30pm Mon-Wed, Fri & Sat, 6.30-10.30pm Sun; 🚉 Ca' d'Oro

Culinary convictions certainly run deep here. Alla Vedova is one of Venice's oldest surviving *osterie*, which explains why you won't find *spritz* (a prosecco-based cocktail) or coffee on the menu, and why you won't pay more than €1 for a bar snack of delicious Venetian meatballs – and it's best not to get the staff started about spaghetti Bolognese. Enjoy superior seasonal *cicheti* at strictly fair prices at the bar, or phone ahead to reserve one of the wood tables that have weathered a thousand elbows in postpasta stupors.

☷ ANICE STELLATO
Inventive Venetian €€

☎ 041 720744; Fondamenta della Sensa 3272; ⏱ 10am-3pm & 7pm-midnight Wed-Sun; 🚉 Madonna dell'Orto

The location may seem obscure, but word has gotten out about Anice Stellato's wild sea bass with aromatic herbs and sea salt, its pistachio-encrusted lamb fillet and its perfectly fried *moeche* (soft-shelled crab). The inspired menu is local and largely organic, with tantalising hints of Venice's historic spice trade, and the staff proudly serve filtered tap water instead of the environmentally unfriendly bottled stuff. Friendliness is the operative word here, with tables set close enough for chatting, waiters you can trust to choose for you, and prices that are lower than you'd expect for daring cuisine of this calibre.

☷ ANTICA ADELAIDE
Classic Venetian €€

☎ 041 5232629; Calle Priuli Racheta; ⏱ noon-3pm & 6-11pm; 🚉 Ca' d'Oro; ⓥ

Impeccable spaghetti with razor clams aside, this menu satisfies even nonpescetarians: vegetarians luxuriate in orechiette ('little ear') pasta with gorgonzola and almonds, and blood-orange-tinged guinea fowl matches the orange-blossom Traminer white.

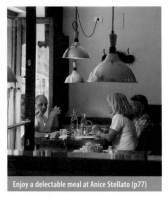
Enjoy a delectable meal at Anice Stellato (p77)

BEA VITA
Inventive Venetian €€

☎ 041 2759347; **Fondamente delle Cappuccine 3082;** ⏱ noon–3pm & 6.30–10.30pm Mon–Sat; 🚉 **Guglie**
With adventurous specials such as pumpkin *sformata* (savoury flan) with goose or steak with a reduction of Valpollicella and wild berries, chef-owners Roberto and Gilberto offer welcome changes from Venetian seafood standards – and their creative €28 three-course prix-fixe and inspired wine pairing put predictable tourist menus and bland house wines to shame.

DA ALBERTO
Cicheti, Classic Venetian €€

☎ 041 5238153; **Calle Larga G Gallina 5401;** ⏱ noon–3pm & 6–10pm Mon–Sat; 🚉 **Ospedale**

This place has all the makings of a true Venetian *osteria* – hidden location, casks of wine, chandeliers that look like medieval torture devices – plus fair prices and a range of seasonal *cicheti* that goes well beyond the usual crostini; dishes include a crispy Venetian seafood fry and salty-sweet *baccalà* (dried cod). Be warned: the kitchen closes early when the joint's not jumping.

LA CANTINA *Cicheti* €€
☎ 041 5228258; **Campo San Felice 3689;** ⏱ 11am–11pm Mon–Sat; 🚉 **Ca' d'Oro**
Damp days are meant for perching on a stool here and warming your face with your bowl of hearty bean soup, while summer scorchers will have you literally over a barrel with microbrewed Morgana beer and heaping bruschette. Food is cooked to order and fish platters worth the wait – think mullet with roast potatoes, sweet *scampi crudi* and corn-breaded fried anchovies.

L'ORTO DEI MORI
Inventive Venetian €€

☎ 041 5243677; **Campo dei Mori 3386;** ⏱ 12.30–3.30pm & 7pm–midnight Wed–Mon; 🚉 **Madonna dell'Orto**
Snug, romantic and modern with dark wood rafters, exposed brick walls and warm hints of orange, this 30-seat hideaway is packed with couples nightly. With such cheerful service, close seating and free-

flowing wine, you may soon find yourself adopted by the Venetian couple next to you. Go with classic scampi risotto, or get creative with squid atop spinach tagliatelle – but have the *bavarese* (Bavarian cream) with glazed chestnuts for dessert. Ask about Thursday wine tastings (€45 per person), led by an English-speaking sommelier.

🍴 OSTERIA BOCCADORO
Inventive Venetian €€€
☎ 041 5211021; www.boccadoro venezia.it; Campiello Widmann 5405a; 🕙 noon-3pm & 7-10pm Tue-Sun; 🚣 Fondamente Nuove

Birds sweetly singing above your table in this bucolic *campo* are probably angling for your leftovers, but they don't stand a chance. Chef/owner Luciano's creative *crudi* (raw seafood) are two-bite delights – tuna with blood orange, sweet prawn atop a sliver of tart green apple – and the cloudlike gnocchi topped with spider crab are gone entirely too soon. Pair your seafood dishes with mineral-rich Traminer white, and save room for a luxuriant dessert: mousse made with six kinds of chocolate.

🍴 VINI DA GIGIO
Classic Venetian €€€
☎ 041 5285140; www.vinidagigio.com; Fondamente San Felice 3628a; 🕙 6.30pm-midnight Wed-Sun; 🚣 Ca' d'Oro

Both boats and time drift past this canalside *osteria* without anyone seeming to notice. Must be the scallops served on the half-shell, drizzled with a wine reduction and accompanied by creamy white polenta, or the choice of 'oh, about a thousand' limited-production wines, all personally recommended by your host and resident research scientist of drink, Paolo Lazzari.

🍸 DRINK
🍸 AL TIMON *Cafe-Bar*
☎ 041 5246066; Fondamente degli Ormesini 2754; 🕙 11am-3pm & 6pm-1am Thu-Tue; 🚣 Guglie

Pull up your director's chair next to the canal and let the show begin. There's a steady parade of been-there-done-that bohemians and starry-eyed students, a massive range of crostini, and enough quality hooch to keep the evening nicely lubricated until the wee hours.

🍸 OSTERIA AGLI ORMESINI
Pub
☎ 041 715834; Fondamente degli Ormesini 2710; 🕙 6.30pm-2am Mon-Sat; 🚣 Madonna dell'Orto

While the rest of the city is awash in wine, beer is the drink of choice here, with 120 mostly foreign brews to choose from. The scene inevitably spills into the street, especially when students descend for *panini* – but try to keep it down

SESTIERI

CANNAREGIO

GIRI DI OMBRE: THREE BOOZY VIEWS OF VENICE

Dorsoduro

The quintessential Venetian *giro di ombra* (happy hour) starts at **Cantinone 'Gia Schiavi'** (p122) with an *ombra* (glass) of wine or *pallottoline* (small bottle of beer). Make a pit stop for a mixed plate of cold cuts, marinated veggies and cheese with a glass of house wine at **Osteria alla Bifora** (p123), or head straight onto a *spritz* (prosecco-based cocktail) at **Caffè Rosso** (p122) or **Imagina Café** (p123). By the time you arrive at **ImprontaCafé** (p120), you'll be ready for grilled polenta with mushrooms – and maybe a bracing espresso.

Rialto

This is the perfect *giro di ombra* for lazy drinkers, since all your hooch options are within a couple of blocks. Start at **I Rusteghi** (p55) for small bar bites served on low courtyard tables with big, full-bodied reds (don't even think about asking for a *spritz* here). Drift over the bridge to **Al Mercà** (p96) for an *ombra* of house wine, then pull up a seat in the piazza to linger over your next glass at **Al Muro** (p96). Finally, roll into **Sacro e Profano** (p94) before the last of the night's speciality pasta is dished out.

Cannaregio

Bar-hop along the waterfront, starting with meatballs and a glass of the good stuff at the bar at **Alla Vedova** (p77). Head onwards and upwards along Rio Terà della Maddalena, through the Ghetto and across the next bridge to **Al Timon** (p79) for some well-earned crostini and a sit-down *ombra* along the canal. Your next move is a tough choice: beer at nearby **Osteria agli Ormesini** (p79), or risotto and reasonable wines at handy **Bea Vita** (p78)? Experienced pub crawlers (you know who you are) already know their answer: both.

to a dull roar, or the neighbours and the management get testy.

▼ UN MONDO DI VINO
Wine Bar
☎ 041 5211093; Salizada San Canzian 5984a; ⏰ 11am-3pm & 6.30-11pm Tue-Sun; 🚢 Rialto

Get there early to grab the fresh bar nosh – marinated artichokes and mussels, if you're lucky – and a few square inches of ledge to

help you balance your plate and glass of wine. There are 45 wines offered by the glass here, and prices range from €1.50 to €3.50, so take a chance on whatever the bartender recommends.

★ PLAY

☆ BOTTEGA DEL TINTORETTO
Course
☎ 041 722081; www.tintorettovenezia .it; Fondamenta dei Mori 3400; 5-day

course incl lunch & materials €390;
🎭 Rialto

Walking the canals of Cannaregio, you're bound to feel an aquatint coming on – and Roberto Mazzetto can show you how to get that out of your system and onto paper. He runs intensive workshops and five-day summer courses in etching and other forms of printmaking, art and design from the *bottega* (workshop) that was once Tintoretto's studio – not a bad pedigree to bring to your next art project.

⭐ CASINO DI VENEZIA *Casino*

☎ 041 5297111; www.casinovenezia.it; Campiello Vendramin 2040; admission €5; 🕑 3pm-2.30am Sun-Thu, 3pm-3am Fri & Sat; 🎭 San Marcuola

Daily dramas at the casino are worthy of their own opera at La Fenice, and that's the way it's been since Venice got the gambling bug in the 16th century. Composer Richard Wagner survived the 20-year effort of writing his stormy *Ring* cycle only to die at the casino in 1883. Jackets are required and strong constitutions advisable if you want to take on the tables here – the high stakes are not for the faint of heart.

⭐ CINEMA GIORGIONE MOVIE D'ESSAI *Cinema*

☎ 041 5226298; Rio Terà di Franceschi 4612; adult/student €7.50/5.50; 🕑 shows 5.30pm, 7.30pm & 10pm; 🎭 Ca' d'Oro

This two-screen cinema has a *Cinema Paradiso* feel about it – it's the only cinema in Venice proper, and audiences arrive en masse, primed for entertainment. Spoiler alert: there's an audible buzz of anticipation around any movie with a good review, so if you understand Italian you may hear the ending while waiting to buy tickets.

⭐ PARADISO PERDUTO *Live Music*

☎ 041 720581; Fondamenta della Misericordia 2540; 🕑 7pm-1am Thu-Mon; 🎭 Madonna dell'Orto

Long tables may make this joint look like a union hall, but it's the right set-up for grog among new friends and for live-music acts that have been known to dissolve into audience-participation jam sessions. Skip the unexceptional food and hit outdoor tables in summer for conversation you can actually hear.

>SAN POLO

Heavenly devotion and earthly delights are neighbours in San Polo, where you'll find both truly divine art and the city's ancient red-light district, now home to artisans' workshops and excellent *osterie* (restaurant-bars). The pride of the *sestiere* (neighbourhood) is a pair of fraternal-twin masterpieces that couldn't be more different: I Frari, with Titian's glowing, gorgeous Madonna; and the Scuola Grande di San Rocco, with its action-packed, turbulent Tintorettos. Foodies can have a different kind of religious experience at the Rialto markets, where mounds of exceptionally fresh seafood and produce look more like offerings to the gods. Photographers elbow drooling gourmets aside to capture glistening fish artfully balanced on their tails atop hillocks of ice, and row after row of exotic vegetables from marshy lagoon gardens. But if it's a retail high you're after, San Polo's artisans' studios will make you think you've died and gone to shopping heaven – without being hell on your wallet.

SAN POLO

SEE

CASA DI GOLDONI

☎ 041 2759325; www.museicivici
veneziani.it; Calle dei Nomboli 2794;
adult/student €2.50/1.50, free with
Museum Pass; ⏰ 10am-6pm Wed-Mon
Apr-Oct, 10am-4pm Wed-Mon Nov-Mar;
🚤 San Tomà

Comedians, musicians and writ-
ers will feel inspiration bubbling
up like a belly laugh from the
stone floors at the birthplace of
Carlo Goldoni (1707–93), creator
of *opera buffa* (comic opera) and
delicious social satires. As the
1st-floor display explains, Goldoni
was a master of second and third
acts: he was a doctor's apprentice
before switching to law, a back-up
career that proved handy when
some comedies didn't sell. But
Goldoni had the last laugh, with
salon sitcoms that made socialites
chuckle at themselves. The main
draws in the museum are the 18th-
century marionettes and puppet
theatre, but don't miss chamber-
music concerts held here; see the
museum's website for a schedule.

CHIESA DI SAN POLO

Campo San Polo 2118; admission €3, with
Chorus pass free; ⏰ 10am-5pm Mon-Sat;
🚤 San Silvestro

This 9th-century Byzantine church
has kept a low profile over the
centuries while housing grew up

around it, so most travellers speed
past without realising it's there.
With a high ship's-keel ceiling and
stained-glass windows from the
14th to 15th centuries, San Polo
is surprisingly airy inside, if a little
dark – and the same is true of the
art. Tintoretto's *Last Supper* is rife
with tension, as apostles react with
outrage, hurt and anger at Jesus'
news that one of them will betray
him. Giandominico Tiepolo (son of
baroque ceiling maestro Giambattista) shows the dark side of hu-
manity in his *Stations of the Cross:*
jeering onlookers torment Jesus,
his blood-stained rags contrasting
with their baroque finery. Literally
and figuratively, Tiepolo lays it
on thickly, so that when a lushly
painted Jesus leaps from his tomb
on the gold ceiling, it's the ultimate
comeuppance for his tormentors.

I FRARI

Chiesa di Santa Maria Gloriosa dei Frari;
Campo dei Frari; admission €3, with
Chorus pass free; ⏰ 9am-6pm Mon-Sat,
1-6pm Sun; 🚤 San Tomà

Is it hot in here, or is it just Titian's
1518 *Madonna of the Assump-
tion* (see p16)? This smouldering
altar masterpiece draws visitors
into the apse and out of this
world, capturing the moment the
Madonna escapes this mortal coil
and reaches heavenward, her signature Titian red robe in glorious
disarray as she finds her footing

Feel your jaw drop (multiple times) at glorious I Frari

on a cloud. Inside the painting, on-lookers below gasp and point out the ascending Madonna to one another – not unlike the modern-day visitors to the church. As if this weren't already too much to handle, the lofty Gothic brick church has other wow-factor features: minuscule puzzlework marquetry in the *coro* (choir stalls), Giovanni Bellini's achingly sweet sacristy triptych, Titian's *Madonna of Ca' Pesaro* to the left of the choir, and the marble-pyramid mausoleum of Antonio Canova, which the artist had originally intended as a monument to Titian. Titian was lost to the plague aged 90 in 1576, but legend has it that, in light of

his contribution to I Frari, the strict rules of quarantine were bent to allow his burial in the church.

☉ PONTE DELLE TETTE
🚇 Rialto

'Tits Bridge' got its name in the late 15th century, when neighbourhood prostitutes were encouraged to display their wares in the windows instead of taking their marketing campaigns to the streets. Crossing over the bridge, you'll reach Rio Terà delle Carampane, named after the house of a noble family (Ca' Rampani) that became notorious as a meeting place for local working girls, who to this day are known as *carampane*.

PONTE DI RIALTO

Rialto

An amazing feat of engineering in its day, Antonio da Ponte's 1592 marble bridge was for centuries the only land link across the Grand Canal. It cost 250,000 gold ducats, a staggering sum that puts cost overruns for the new Ponte di Calatrava (p102) into perspective. Now that the Rialto is clogged with kiosks and foot-traffic jams, locals go out of their way to avoid it, or zip up the less scenic northern side of the bridge. The southern side faces San Marco and, after the crowds of shutterbugs and tour groups clear out around sunset, it offers panoramas of a picturesque stretch of the Grand Canal lined with *palazzi* (palaces or mansions).

SCUOLA GRANDE DI SAN ROCCO

☎ 041 5234864; www.scuolagrande sanrocco.it; Campo San Rocco 3052; adult/under 26yr €7/5; ☿ 9.30am-5.30pm; ⛴ San Tomà

Tintoretto's masterpiece took 23 years to complete (1575–87), but it's so fresh and immediate you'd swear the paint is still wet. Everyone wanted the commission to paint this building, dedicated to the patron saint of the plague stricken, so Tintoretto had to produce something exceptional – and, just to be sure he won, he

cheated a little. Instead of producing sketches like his rival Paolo Veronese, Tintoretto painted a ceiling piece and dedicated it to the saint – knowing the confraternity couldn't refuse an offering to San Rocco, and that other painters would have to work around the piece. Tintoretto went all out in the upstairs Sala Grande Superiore, covering the walls with action-packed biblical scenes that read like a graphic novel. This painting cycle seems to come with its own sound effects: you can almost hear the *swoop!* overhead as an angel dives down to feed an ailing Elijah. Unlike the Venetian colourists, Tintoretto concentrated on dynamic lines, and you can see the roots of modern abstract expressionism in *Agony in the Garden,* where a sketchy, anxious Jesus faces his fate against a black, X-shaped void. See p15 for more on Tintoretto.

🛍 SHOP

ATTOMBRI *Jewellery*

☎ 041 5212524; www.attombri.com; Sottoportico degli Oresi 74, Rialto; ☿ 9am-1pm & 3-7pm Mon-Sat; ⛴ Rialto

Dolce&Gabbana models recently worked Attombri designs on Milan catwalks; now you too can strut the Rialto in this dramatic, handcrafted jewellery. Stefano and Daniele Attombri bend wire into waves, which then curl around the wrist with lagoon green beads, or grace the collarbone with red-beaded starfish. Prices start at around €40, making these accessories a steal compared to a D&G tee.

🏠 BOTTEGA DEGLI ANGELI
Ceramics
☎ 041 710866; www.bottegangeli.com; Calle del Cristo 2224; 🕙 10am-1pm & 3-8pm Mon-Sat; 🚊 Rialto

Huge vases, smallish tiles, tiny pendants: there's something to suit every taste and carry-on limit here. The work of the three resident ceramists ranges from stark, dramatic shapes to abstract stained-glass patterns and even whimsical fish, but the signature is a bright red glaze that (as any ceramist will tell you) is quite difficult to achieve. The shop doubles as a studio, with mother-daughter ceramists Silvia and Giulia Ferretti working behind the counter.

🏠 CAMPIELLO CA' ZEN
Antiques
☎ 041 714871; www.campiellocazen .com; Campiello Zen 2581; 🕙 9am-1pm & 3-7pm Mon-Sat; 🚊 San Tomà

An antique glass lamp would be the last thing you'd want to cram in your luggage – or so you thought before you saw the 1940s Salviati silvery bluebell chandelier and the ultramod Scarpa table lamps. That fabulous hand-blown chalice

seems downright practical by comparison. But here's a dangerous thought: Campiello Ca' Zen ships.

🏠 CARTÉ *Paper Crafts*
☎ 320 0248776; Calle di Cristi 1731; 🕙 9am-1pm & 3-7.30pm Mon-Sat; 🚊 San Tomà

Paperwork never seemed such a good idea. After years of restoring ancient manuscripts and books, Rosanna Corró (p76) decided to put those skills to work making something entirely original, and she's been on a roll ever since. This tiny shop is packed with must-have paper-and-clothbound purses in lagoon-ripple patterns; peacock-eye marbled paper panels that bring Venetian glamour to your living room walls; swirly op-art jewellery boxes that outshine their contents; and marbled wood-grain albums and journals that will do justice to your Venice trip.

🏠 DROGHERIA MASCARI
Food, Wine
☎ 041 5229762; Ruga degli Spezieri 381; 🕙 8am-1pm & 4-7.30pm Mon, Tue & Thu-Sat, 8am-1pm Wed; 🚊 San Silvestro

Food is the drug of choice at this historic spice merchant, where wares are still dispensed from banks of tiny wooden drawers and copper-topped jars. Window displays feature ziggurat-shaped

Feed your imagination at Drogheria Mascari (p87)

piles of cayenne and leaning towers of star anise alongside bio-dynamic Veneto wines and estate-grown olive oils. For an impressive selection of Italian wines starting at €5.50, don't miss the *enoteca* (wine store) out the back.

FANNY *Leather Goods*
☎ 041 5228266; Calle dei Saoneri 2723; 🕙 10am-7.30pm; 🚊 San Tomà

Quit snickering about the name – when that Venice chill hits your extremities, you'll be seriously glad you found this treasure trove of leather gloves. No need to sacrifice style for warmth here: check out the purple pair with tiny yellow buttons, or those cashmere-lined

turquoise numbers. At these prices, splashy orange wrist-strap clutches and spring green leather handbags are tempting add-on sales.

GILBERTO PENZO
Model Boats
☎ 041 719372; www.veniceboats.com; Calle 2 dei Saoneri 2681; 🕙 9am-12.30pm & 3-6pm Mon-Sat; 🚊 San Tomà

Yes, you actually can take a gondola home in your pocket. Anyone fascinated by the models at the Museo Storico Navale (p62) will go wild here amid handmade wooden models of all kinds of Venetian boats, including some that are seaworthy (or, at least, bathworthy). For crafty types, Signore Penzo creates kits so you can have a crack at it yourself.

HIBISCUS *Fashion*
☎ 041 5208989; Ruga Rialto 1060; 🕙 10am-7pm Mon-Sat, 11am-7pm Sun; 🚊 San Tomà

Caught in Venice without a stitch to wear to a Biennale opening? You can either hope for a fairy godmother or head straight to Hibiscus. Venice's creative crossroads style is built here piece by distinctive piece: a black and white jacket diagonally striped to create an optical-illusion nipped-in waist, Japanese silk socks with gossamer flowers, and a locally made ceramic-disc necklace.

▣ I VETRI A LUME DI AMADI
Glass

☎ 041 5238089; Calle Saoneri 2747;
⏱ 9am-12.30pm & 3-6pm Mon-Fri,
3-6pm Sat; 🚊 San Silvestro

Glass menageries don't get more fascinating than the one created before your eyes by Signore Amadi. Sea anemones with glowing pink-tipped tentacles and fierce little glass crabs waving their claws are just the beginning of the wonders here: check out the medicine cabinet display of eerily lifelike glass mosquitoes, balancing on spindly legs the width of a hair. The remarkable blue glass horses look like Picasso drawings in three dimensions, and the glass beans and spring onions may leave you craving vegetables for lunch.

▣ IL BAULE BLU *Antiques, Toys*
☎ 041 719448; San Tomà 2915a;
⏱ 10.30am-12.30pm & 4-7.30pm Mon-Sat; 🚊 San Tomà

On recent inspection, this curiosity cabinet of elusive treasures included antique Steiff teddy bears, vintage Murano *murrine* (glass beads), a swingy green polka-dot Marni skirt and a wide selection of bug-eyed vintage sunglasses. If travel has proved tough on your kid's favourite toy, first aid and kind words will be administered at the in-house teddy hospital.

▣ IL GUFO ARTIGIANO
Leather Goods

☎ 041 5234030; Ruga del Speziali 299;
⏱ 10am-3.30pm Mon-Sat; 🚊 Rialto

Venice pictures demand a suitable album, and here you can have your pick of leather ones embossed by hand in glowing colours made with vegetable dyes. The swirling designs – which are also embossed onto journals, handbags and wallets – come from ironwork on Venetian windows, but are combined with abstract modern flair.

▣ LA BOTTEGA DI GIO
Jewellery

☎ 041 714664; www.labottegadigio.it; Fondamenta dei Frari 2559a; ⏱ 10am-1pm & 3-7pm Mon-Sat; 🚊 San Tomà

The glass necklaces in the shops not quite your style? Make your own with genuine Murano glass beads and your choice of coloured wire, silk thread or leather cord at this DIY jewellery shop. Lampwork beads begin at €1, and one or two may be all you need for a highly original Venice souvenir.

▣ MILLE E UNA NOTA
Musical Instruments

☎ 041 5231822; Calle di Mezzo 1235;
⏱ 9.45am-1pm & 3.30-7.30pm Mon-Sat;
🚊 San Tomà

The same thought occurs to almost everyone after hearing

While in Venice, pick up some stunning handmade paper products

Interpreti Veneziani (p56): is it too late to take up an instrument? The easiest option would be the harmonica, and Mille e Una Note has an impressive range of vintage and modern ones from the Italian Alps and Switzerland. But, if you're feeling very ambitious, you can pick up some Albinoni sheet music and a lute here too.

PIED À TERRE *Shoes*
☎ 041 5285513; www.piedaterre
-venice.com; Sottoportico degli Oresi 60;
🕙 10am-1pm & 3-7pm Tue-Sat, 3-7pm
Mon; 🚊 Rialto

Though 18th-century Rialto courtesans started a craze for 30cm-high heels, the fashion for slippers never left Venice. Pied à Terre's colourful baroque Venetian *furlane* (slippers) are handcrafted in velvet and silk, with recycled bicycle tyre treads ideal for finding your footing on a gondola.

SABBIE E NEBBIE
Gifts, Homewares
☎ 041 719073; Calle dei Nomboli 2768a;
🕙 10am-12.30pm & 4-7.30pm Mon-Sat;
🚊 San Tomà

The latest East–West trade-route trends begin here, with Japanese-inspired Rina Menardi ceramics, woven opera wraps made in India and handmade books from Bologna created with Japanese paper-marbling techniques.

🏠 VIZIOVIRTÙ *Chocolate*
☎ 041 2750149; www.viziovirtu.com;
Calle de Campaniel 2898a; 🕙 10am-
6.30pm Mon-Sat; 🚇 San Tomà
Try some of Venice's most decadent vices and tasty virtues at this
extraordinary chocolate shop. As if
the hot-chocolate fountain weren't
enough of a Willy Wonka–esque
attraction, the filled chocolates
here come in a five-course meal
of flavours: blueberry and violet,
barolo wine, redcurrant and
basil, balsamic vinegar, and 'Freud'
(which tastes like a cigar, naturally).

🏠 ZAZU *Fashion*
☎ 041 715426; Calle dei Saoneri 2750;
🕙 2.30-7.30pm Mon, 9.30am-1.30pm &
2.30-7.30pm Tue-Sat; 🚇 San Tomà
Be the fashion world's Ms Marco
Polo with your Italian-designed
tapestry bags, one-of-a-kind dresses from Barcelona and Japanese
wrap tops. Prices are above sports-
wear but below couture, and the
sale rack in the back usually has
great pieces for €50 to €100.

🍴 EAT
🍴 ALL'ARCO *Cicheti*   €€
☎ 041 5205666; Calle dell'Arco 436;
🕙 noon-3.30pm Mon-Sat Oct-Mar,
noon-8.30pm Apr-Jun & Sep, closed Jul &
Aug; 🚇 San Silvestro
'I want what she's having…' is
always the right order at All'Arco,
where the best *cicheti* (Venetian
tapas) in town aren't on the menu,
and technically don't even have
a name. Maestro Francesco (see
p93) and his son Matteo make
them up daily, with Francesco
commandeering the kitchen's tiny
burners to turn out one of his 'fan-
tasias' of grilled prawns with white
asparagus tips wrapped in pancetta and sage, while Matteo takes
over after Saturday fish deliveries
to invent a tuna tartare with mint,
strawberries and a balsamic reduction. Even with copious prosecco,
hardly any meal devoured at the
bar ever tops €20 or falls short of
four stars – you might as well book
your return ticket to Venice now.

🍴 ANTICA BIRRERIA LA
CORTE *Pizza*   €€
☎ 041 2750570; Campo San Polo 2168;
🕙 noon-11pm; 🚇 San Silvestro
This former bullfight pen became
a brewery in the 19th century to
keep Venice's Austrian occupiers
occupied, and now it's a modern
eatery featuring (you guessed it)
grilled beef and good beer. Pizza
is the way to go here, including
such nontouristy versions as
rocket, bresaola (air-dried beef)
and grana padano. With room for
150, there's hardly ever a wait,
and the piazza seating is perfect
for outdoor movie screenings
and live-theatre performances in
summer.

🍴 ANTICHE CARAMPANE
Classic Venetian €€€

☎ 041 5240165; www.antichecaram pane.com; Rio Terà delle Carampane 1911; ⏰ 7-11pm Tue-Sat; 🚉 San Stae
Hidden in the former red-light dis-trict behind Ponte delle Tette (Tits Bridge), this culinary indulgence is a bit of a trick to find. Cheap it's not, and you may wonder who you have to, erm, know to get a reser-vation – but the recited daily menu of velvety carpaccio, asparagus and crab salad and spicy seafood pasta are Rialto-fresh specials you won't find on tourist menus.

🍴 ANTICO PANIFICIO *Pizza* €

☎ 041 2770967; Campiello del Sol 929; ⏰ bakery noon-3pm & 7-11pm Thu-Mon, restaurant noon-3pm & 7-11pm Wed-Mon; 🚉 San Silvestro; Ⓥ
Most Venetian pizzerias pander to tourists, but this spot is a local in-stitution. Outdoor seating is always packed, so be prepared to lunge at free tables and order decisively. Basic choices such as margherita (with basil, mozzarella and tomato) insult the chef's intelligence – go with anchovies, zucchini flowers or whatever topping your neighbours are enjoying.

🍴 DAI ZEMEI *Cicheti* €

☎ 041 5208546; www.ostariadaizemei .it; Ruga Vecchia San Giovanni 1045; ⏰ 9am-8pm; 🚉 San Silvestro

The twins (*zemei,* hence the name of this place) who run this corner joint are a blur of motion by 10am, preparing for the onslaught of regulars and the odd well-informed foodie tourist. The toasted bruschette are usually the first to go along with the lard-and-rocket *panini* (sandwiches), but there's always a good range of crostini, including gorgonzola with walnuts and a brandy reduction. Think past the usual prosecco and wash it down with a rustic raboso or sophisti-cated refosco.

🍴 MAURO EL FORNER DE CANTON *Bread & Pastries* €

☎ 041 5222890; Ruga Vecchia di San Giovanni 603; ⏰ 7am-7pm Mon-Sat; 🚉 Rialto; Ⓥ
Stop at this bakery and patisserie to fill any pressing picnic needs that haven't already been met by the Rialto produce markets (see p94) for sunny lunches down by the dock. Carbo-load in style with golden grissini (thin, crisp breadsticks), the ubiquitous *bovoli* (snail-shaped rolls), crusty baguettes and, to add some fibre to a pasta-centric diet, whole-grain breads. Sweet standouts here include cream puffs, flaky *sfoglie di mele* (apple tarts), and delicious hazelnut *pan dei dogi* (nut-studded biscuits) as rich as a doge.

Francesco Pinto
Maestro of cicheti (Venetian tapas) at All'Arco (p91) and third-generation osteria (restaurant-bar) impresario

Why there's no menu It's like Venice: there are some common themes and ingredients, but the rest is pure fantasy, and what you find today might not be here tomorrow. I'm more of a traditionalist, but my son Matteo makes modern dishes, Italian *crudi* [composed bites of raw fish] with a creative touch like a sushi chef. Cooking isn't work, it's something we do for fun.
Don't leave Venice without tasting… *Sarde in saor* [sardines in an onion marinade] and *baccalà mantecato* [mashed cod prepared in garlic and parsley], not made industrially but with dried cod that is soaked for 48 hours. Try ancient Venetian dishes like *nervetti* [calf's tendons] and *trippa* [tripe]… *[interrupts himself]* Do you smell that? Somebody's cooking squid. *Seppioline in nero* [squid cooked in its own ink], you must try that…you'd better stay awhile. **How to thank the cook** Just come and eat well. Stay an hour, give us time to invent some new dish for you. That's gratification enough.

SESTIERI

SAN POLO

🍴 PASTICCERIA RIZZARDINI
Pastries €
☎ 041 5223835; Campiello dei Meloni 1415; 🕑 7.30am-8pm Wed-Mon; 🚊 San Silvestro

'From 1742' reads the modest storefront sign, and inside you'll find the secret weapons that have helped this little bakery last so long: killer cream puffs and dangerous doughnuts. Trawl the biscuit section in search of wagging *lingue di suocere* (mother-in-law's tongues), *pallone di Casanova* (Casanova's balls) and other *dolci tipici Venexiani* (typical Venetian sweets), but act fast if you want that last slice of tiramisu.

🍴 PESCHERIA *Self-Catering*
Rialto; 🕑 7am-2pm; 🚊 Rialto

Slinging fresh fish daily for 700 years and still going strong, the fishmongers here are more vital to Venetian cuisine than any chef. Ask how and where a seafood delicacy was caught, and you'll get an earful about recent shifts in Adriatic aquaculture. Sustainable fishing is not new here: marble plaques show regulations set centuries ago for minimum allowable sizes for various types of fish. See also p14.

🍴 PRONTO PESCE PRONTO
Cicheti €€
☎ 041 8220298; Pescheria, Rialto 319; 🕑 12.45-2.45pm; 🚊 Rialto

The fish at the Pescheria (left) look so good you might want to eat them raw – and you can do just that at this fish store that prepares delightful *crudi* (composed bites of raw fish) and lightly dressed seafood salads. There's a counter for leaning on and prosecco for washing it down but, to bump your lunch up a star, take that *folpeti* (baby-octopus) salad and naturally sweet raw-prawn *crudi* down to the dock by the Grand Canal.

🍴 RIALTO PRODUCE MARKETS *Self-Catering*
Rialto; 🕑 7am-3.30pm; 🚊 Rialto

Getting your daily servings of fruit and veg is easy here – you'll be tempted by tantalising teetering pyramids of colourful produce. Salad cravings are a given when you're surrounded by juicy tomatoes, aromatic greens and, in season, tender *castraure* (baby artichokes). Vendors are used to visitors looking and photographing rather than buying, but if you're in the market for picnic makings they might offer you samples. See also p14.

🍴 SACRO E PROFANO
Italian, International €
☎ 041 5237924; Ramo Terzo del Parangon 502; 🕑 11.30am-1pm & 6.30pm-1am Mon, Tue & Thu-Sat, 11.30am-2pm Sun; 🚊 Rialto; Ⓥ

DIY DINNERS: SOME ASSEMBLY REQUIRED

When nothing on the menu seems to hit the mark, you can always assemble a meal to your liking in Venice's markets. If you missed the **Rialto produce markets** (p14, opposite) in full swing in the morning, stop by the **floating farmers market** (Map pp110–11, D3; Campo San Barnaba, Dorsoduro), docked alongside Campo San Barnaba. A warning, though: the produce-barge vendor is a grumpy character who sometimes insists on 500g minimum purchases, knowing you won't be able to resist those piles of tomatoes and blood oranges. Nearby is the **Dorsoduro produce market** (Map pp110–11, D2; Campo Santa Margherita, Dorsoduro), where during the week you'll spot vegetable and fruit stalls, and a small, cheerful fish market oozing squid ink onto the flagstones. If takeaway is more your style, head for the deli counter and bakery at **Coop** (p105), or to **Pronto Pesce Pronto** (opposite) for seafood dishes to go. For something to wash it all down, bring your empty water bottle and fill 'er up straight from the barrel at **Nave d'Oro** (⏰ 8.30am–1pm & 4.30–7.30pm Mon, Tue, Thu–Sat), the wine dispensary with locations in Cannaregio (Map pp72–3, D4, F5), Castello (Map pp60–1, A2, B2) and Dorsoduro (Map pp110–11, D2).

Now the question is 'Where to eat?' Picnicking in Venetian piazzas and *calli* (streets) is forbidden, but you can head to the beaches on the **Lido** (p134), the gardens at the **Biennale pavilions** (p59), the courtyard at your B&B or hostel, or your hotel balcony overlooking the Grand Canal (lucky you) for lunch with a Venetian view.

There's an eclectic crowd and menu at this boho hangout in the Rialto's shadow, run by a member of local cult ska band, Pitura Freska. Strike up conversation over wine and *cicheti* in the *calle,* then head indoors for heaping plates of chicken curry or seasonal vegetarian pastas, all at starving-artist prices – plus occasional outbursts into poetry and song for free entertainment.

🍴 SNACK BAR AI NOMBOLI
Sandwiches €
☎ 041 5230995; Rio Terà dei Nomboli 271c; ⏰ 8am–8pm Mon-Sat; 🚣 San Tomà
This snappy Venetian comeback to McDonald's has scrumptious

crusty rolls filled with local cheeses; savoury salami, prosciutto, roast beef and other cold cuts; roast vegetables and sprightly greens that are more than garnishes; and condiments ranging from spicy mustard to wild-nettle sauce. Two sandwiches is a filling lunch; three is a proper feast.

🍴 TRATTORIA DA IGNAZIO
Classic Venetian €€
☎ 041 5234852; Calle Saoneri 2749; ⏰ noon-3pm & 7-11pm Mon-Sat; 🚣 San Silvestro
Old-school charm is the key here: grilled lagoon fish and homemade pasta ('of course') are served

with a proud flourish by dapper, well-fed waiters, who know they're providing good quality at a fair price. The cheerful dining room with yellow linens and orchids on every table is pretty enough, but on sunny days and warm nights the entire neighbourhood converges beneath the grape arbour in the garden.

Y DRINK

Y AL MERCÀ *Wine Bar*
☎ 393 9924781; Campo Bella Vienna 213; 🕓 noon-3pm & 4-9pm Mon-Sat; 🚇 Rialto

The night is young and so is Al Mercà's clientele, who nurse wine or beer as they catch up with old friends they haven't seen since this time yesterday and scrap dinner plans in favour of *cicheti*. Wine by the glass ranges from €2 to €3.50, and *cicheti* start at just €1 for meatballs and mini *panini*. Arrive by 6.30pm for the best selection and easy bar access, or you'll constantly be repeating *'permesso'* (pardon) as you squeeze through the spillover crowd in the piazza.

Y AL MURO
Cocktail Bar, Wine Bar
☎ 041 2412339; Campo Bella Vienna 222; 🕓 9am-3pm & 5pm-1am Mon-Sat, 5pm-1am Sun; 🚇 Rialto

There's no velvet rope here, though it's the kind of place you'd

expect to find one, given the aluminium bar, sexy lighting and see-and-be-seen picture windows. But the prices are still refreshingly friendly, with wines by the glass starting at €2 and respectable cocktails from €5. The upstairs restaurant may be pricier, but the place to be here is by the bar for *cicheti* or at a low table out in the square for late-night drinks.

Y DO MORI *Wine Bar*
☎ 041 5225401; Sotoportego dei do Mori 429; 🕓 8.30am-8pm Mon-Sat; 🚇 Rialto

Behind the kiosk-strewn tourist thoroughfare to the Rialto lurks this sultry backstreet beauty from another era, with its gleaming, gargantuan copper pots and incongruously dainty sandwiches called *francobolli* (literally 'postage stamps'). Come early for the best selection of *cicheti* and local gossip.

Y GINGER *Lounge*
☎ 041 5243808; Fondamenta di Forner 2924; 🕓 8am-midnight Mon-Sat; 🚇 San Tomà

Architect Tadao Ando would appreciate the artful repurposing and minimalist design of this new canalside lounge, which echoes his Punta della Dogana redesign with exposed brick walls and an open plan for an easy flow of light and conversation. All that style, yet the wine menu rarely tops €5 – even for top-notch Tocai and small-producer soave – and there's beer on tap and *panini* aplenty.

⭐ PLAY

⭐ SCUOLA GRANDE DI SAN GIOVANNI EVANGELISTA
Classical Music

☎ 041 4266559; www.scuolasan giovanni.it; Campo della Scuola 2454; adult €30-35, student €20-25; 🕑 concert 8.30pm Tue, Thu & Sun; 🚊 Ferrovia

Perennial Italian opera favourites – Puccini's *Tosca,* Verdi's *La Traviata,* Rossini's *Il Barbiere di Seviglia* – are performed by local opera troupes in the highly operatic setting of the Scuola Grande di San Giovanni Evangelista. This Venetian confraternity long included members of the dreaded Council of Ten, Venice's secret service, making it one of the most powerful and well-endowed Venetian institutions – and now that the restored palace is open for concerts, you can watch melodramas unfold in the backrooms where history was made. Enter the courtyard through Pietro Lombardo's 1481 triumphal arch for a sense of heady importance no mere red carpet can convey. Sweep up the grand double 15th-century staircase designed by Mauro Codussi to your concert venue: Giorgio Massari's 1729 Scuola meeting hall, lined with paintings by Giandomenico Tiepolo. Not bad for an evening's entertainment.

⭐ SUMMER ARENA
Cinema, Theatre

Campo San Polo; 🕑 Jul & Aug; 🚊 San Tomà

In summer ancient Campo San Polo becomes the forward thinking Summer Arena, with free open-air cinema, concerts and theatre performances. This space is wide open to ideas year-round, however, so watch out for political rallies and impromptu rave sessions.

>SANTA CROCE

So this is how Venice lives when it's not busy entertaining. Santa Croce is a network of winding lanes lined with artisans' studios, *campi* (squares) where kids tear around on tricycles while adults sip prosecco, pizza joints that are cheap enough for teenagers on dates, alternative-culture outposts and (since this is Venice, after all) a couple of charmingly quirky museums in historic *palazzi* (palaces or mansions). When the Rialto scene gets too overwhelming, wander west through Santa Croce past Byzantine churches and baroque houses, stopping frequently for outstanding gelato (perennial local favourite: pistachio). Beyond the museums and a couple of churches, there's not much here of major tourist interest, which is what makes it an ideal place to really unwind. No traffic or souvenir salespeople here; instead, there's just the murmur of idle chatter in backstreet *bacari* (restaurant-bars), water lapping at the canal banks, and unhurried footsteps along single-file *calli* (streets).

SANTA CROCE

👁 SEE
Ca' Pesaro **1** H2
Palazzo Mocenigo **2** G2
Ponte di Calatrava **3** B3

🏠 SHOP
CartaVenezia **4** G3
Derò **5** C4
Ervas **6** G3
Mare di Carta **7** C3

🍴 EAT
Ae Oche **8** F3
Al Nono Risorto **9** H3
Al Vecio Pozzo **10** D3
Alaska Gelateria **11** E2
Coop **12** B3
Coop **13** F2
Gelateria San Stae **14** G2
Muro Pizza & Cucina ..**15** G3
Osteria La Zucca **16** F2
Osteria Mocenigo **17** G2
Vecio Fritolin **18** G3

🍸 DRINK
Al Prosecco **19** F2
La Rivetta **20** D3

⭐ PLAY
Casa del Cinema **21** G2

Please see over for map

⦿ SEE

⦿ CA' PESARO

☎ 041 721127; www.museicivicivene
ziani.it; Fondamenta di Ca' Pesaro
2070; adult/EU 6-14yr, student & senior
€6.50/4, free with Museum Pass;
🕑 10am-6pm Tue-Sun Apr-Oct, 10am-
5pm Tue-Sun Nov-Mar; 🚊 San Stae

This highly eccentric museum is a
three-in-one special: modern art
plus Japanese antiques, all in a 1710
Baldassare Longhena–designed
palazzo. The ground-floor Galleria d'Arte Moderna begins with
the shamelessly self-promoting
early days of the Biennale, and its
emphasis on Venetian landscapes,
Venetian painters (notably Giacomo
Favretto) and socialites who sup-
posedly embodied mythological
virtues. But the savvy Biennale
foundation bought key works from
other national pavilions too –
notably Klimt's 1909 *Judith II
(Salome)* and Chagall's *Rabbi of
Vitebsk* (1914–22). The Pesaro family
commissioned the 1901 portrait of
grande dame Letizia from future
futurist Giacomo Balla, while the
1961 De Lisi bequest added Kan-
dinskys and Morandis to the mix.
Upstairs is the wonderfully quirky
Museo Orientale, the result of an
1887–9 shopping spree across
Asia by Prince Enricodi Borbone.
He reached Japan when Edo art
was being discounted in favour

Find a window in your schedule: with art, antiques and architecture, Ca' Pesaro is a one-stop culture shop

A black-and-red colour scheme never dates

of modern Meiji, and his Edo-era swords, miniature sculptures, musical instruments and lacquerware writing sets are highlights of this collection of 30,000 objets d'art.

PALAZZO MOCENIGO
☎ 041 721798; www.museicivicivenez iani.it; Salizada di San Stae 1992; adult/ EU 6-14yr, student & senior €4.50/3, free with Museum Pass; 🕙 10am-5pm Tue-Sun Apr-Oct, 10am-4pm Tue-Sun Nov-Mar; 🚤 San Stae
Fashionistas and fans of costume drama shouldn't miss this museum of textiles, housed in the swanky 18th-century salons of a Gothic Grand Canal palace. It's easy to imagine romance blossoming under the ceiling fresco in the green drawing room, and elections of the doge (Venice's leader) being negotiated in the count's library – seven Mocenigo family members served as dogi. Each room features appropriate garments: a lethal-looking corset in the contessa's bedroom, English-influenced damask rose gowns with plunging necklines in the red living room, and silver-embroidered pink silk socks providing genteel camouflage in the Salmon Dining Room.

PONTE DI CALATRAVA
🚤 Ferrovia, Piazzale Roma
Although it had only just opened when this book went to print, the Calatrava Bridge has already been called many things: a fish tail, a fantasy, unnecessary, overdue, pleasingly streamlined and displeasingly wheelchair inaccessible. There are, however, two things that everyone agrees on: it was expensive and it was late. Budgeted at around €4 million in 2001, the cost of the bridge trebled as engineers corrected a 4cm tolerance that raised questions about its stability. Decide for yourself if the time and money paid off – then join the ongoing debates at happy hour across Venice.

SHOP

CARTAVENEZIA *Paper Crafts*
☎ 041 5241283; www.cartavenezia
.it; Calle Lunga 2125; ⏰ 3.30-7.30pm
Mon, 11am-1pm & 3.30-7.30pm Tue-Sat;
🚊 San Stae

Paper is really put through the
wringer here – but instead of
marbling it, as has been the
custom in Venice for about 150
years, Cartavenezia embosses
and sculpts its handmade cotton
paper. Ancient techniques meet
modern industrial chic in the
striped raw-edged bowls and
lampshades, moulded-paper
jewellery embellished with steel,
and abstract friezes that demand
prime placement in urban lofts.

DERÒ *Ceramics, Glass*
☎ 041 2440074; www.riflessidivenezia
.it; Campazzo Tolentini 200b; ⏰ 10am-
7.30pm; 🚊 Piazzale Roma

Notwithstanding the effusive
efforts of poets and legions of
hyper-stimulated photographers,
Venice remains an elusive city to
capture on paper – so Alessandro
de Rossi opts for glass, wood
and fabric instead. His fanciful
works capture the unmistakable
East-meets-West skyline in series
of quick, calligraphic flourishes
on conveniently portable scarves,
plates and treasure boxes. Seen as
a series of indigo-ink curlicues on
a plain wood backdrop, the city

resembles a long-lost Silk Road
language emerging from the sea.

ERVAS *Textiles, Ironwork*
☎ 041 5200490; www.ervas-venezia
.it; Calle Lunga 2137; ⏰ 10am-1pm &
2.30-7pm Mon-Sat; 🚊 San Stae

A tiny studio packed with Italian
handicrafts, including linens
stamped with whimsical retro-
1970s designs using woodblock-
printing methods that date back
centuries. Bandy-legged lagoon
birds perch on tea-towels, and
bees seem flustered by giant
yellow daisies sprawling across
tablecloths. Ervas' ironwork
studio/showroom across the
calle features must-haves for
your medieval castle or nautically
themed beach-house, including
hand-wrought fireplace tools and
gondola prows.

MARE DI CARTA
Books, Boating Aids
☎ 041 716304; www.maredicarta
.com; Fondamenta dei Tolentini 222;
⏰ 9am-1pm & 3.30-7.30pm Mon-Sat;
🚊 Ferrovia

Sailors and armchair seafarers will
geek out with utter glee at this
store, which is packed with every
map and DIY aid you could possibly need for lagoon exploration,
boat upkeep and spotting local
sealife. If you're considering rowing
lessons or a boat purchase – and

who doesn't after a few days on the lagoon? – stop here first and get informed; you can also pick up a schedule of boating classes offered through the store.

🍴 EAT

🍴 AE OCHE *Pizza* €
☎ 041 5241161; www.aeoche.com; Calle del Tintor 1552a; 🕑 noon-2.20pm & 7-10.30pm Mon-Fri, noon-2.20pm & 7-11.30pm Sat & Sun; 🚊 San Stae; Ⓥ
Champ Louisiana sweet potatoes and Long-Distance Sodas are advertised on vintage signs here, but both the crowd and the 70-pizza menu are modern Venetian. Daredevils order the *equino* (horse meat with lemon) or *mangiafuoco* ('fire-eater'; hot salami, capsicum and tabasco), but perennial favourites are the *tonnata* (tuna, capers and onions) and *estiva* (rocket, seasoned grana padano and cherry tomatoes).

🍴 AL NONO RISORTO
Classic Venetian, Pizza €€
☎ 041 5241169; Sottoportego della Siora Bettina; 🕑 noon-3pm & 6-10pm Fri-Tue, 6-10pm Thu; 🚊 San Stae; Ⓥ
Manifesto or menu? At Al Nono Risorto, pizzas are listed alongside urgent action alerts: 'No abandoning animals! More rights for gays and domestic partners!' Prices are left of centre, radical-chic servers can't be bothered with petty

bourgeois orders and, on sunny days, all of Venice converges on the garden for squid with polenta, bargain house prosecco and political bonding.

🍴 AL VECIO POZZO *Pizza* €€
☎ 041 5242760; www.veciopozzo.it; Campo de Lana 656; 🕑 12.30-2.30pm & 7pm-1am Thu-Tue; 🚊 Ferrovia
Every Venetian quarter once had its own well, where neighbours would gather to gossip on balmy evenings – and now in a square still graced with a *vecio pozzo* (old well), this pizzeria serves the same purpose. Come early for prime seating in the square or settle for sociable tables indoors beneath low-slung rafters, with an illusionistic *campo* (square) scene painted along one wall. Pizzas are a house speciality, but the wood-fired oven yields respectable bruschette and grilled meats, and fresh pasta and tiramisu are made on the premises.

🍴 ALASKA GELATERIA
Gelato, Sustainable Eating €
☎ 041 715211; Calle Larga dei Bari 1159; 🕑 9am-1pm & 3-8pm; 🚊 Riva de Biasio
Kids may like their ice cream blue and with gum balls, but foodies prefer theirs organic and with flashes of culinary brilliance – and Alaska delivers. Taste buds

applaud the roasted-pistachio gelato, but are confounded by the *carciofi*. Could that savoury, barely sweet cream with a subtle minty flavour really be *artichoke*? Yes – and it's stunning paired with the tangy lemon. Cardamom and dark chocolate with orange peel is not your standard combo, but at just €1.80 for a double cone, you can afford such culinary risks.

🍴 COOP *Self-Catering*
☎ 041 2960621; Piazzale Roma; ⏰ 9am-1pm & 4-7.30pm Mon-Sat; 🚊 Piazzale Roma

Find yourself a *campo* or canalside spot and enjoy an exceptional picnic with supplies from Coop, a supermarket that has prime take-away, basics and biscuits, all under enticing spotlighting. The branch at Piazzale Rome is the biggest supermarket in the city centre, and its olive and meat selections are sublime. There's another branch at Campo San Giacomo dell'Orio.

🍴 GELATERIA SAN STAE
Gelato €

☎ 041 710689; www.gelateriasanstae.com; Salizada di San Stae 1910; ⏰ 11am-9pm Tue-Sun; 🚊 San Stae

Simple flavours are anything but at San Stae, where the signature ingredients – ranging from Piedmont hazelnut to Madagascar vanilla – are gathered from near and far. Happiness is at hand with €1.50 cones, but heaven is a €2 double with strawberry and prosecco flavours.

🍴 MURO PIZZA & CUCINA
Pizza €€

☎ 041 5241628; www.murovenezia.com; Campiello dello Spezier 2048; ⏰ noon-11pm Wed-Mon; 🚊 San Stae

Mellow at lunch, trendy at happy hour and chic at dinner: this versatile restaurant bar-pizzeria aims to please. Grab a chair in the piazza, or duck into the snug exposed-brick interior for prime seating on white-leather-and-striped-silk banquettes. Inventive pizza makes a reasonable-but-not-overly-cheap date, lighting is shamelessly flattering, and the beer and wine selection is above average – sounds like a recipe for romance, no?

🍴 OSTERIA LA ZUCCA
Mediterranean €€

☎ 041 5241570; www.lazucca.it; Calle del Tentor 1762; ⏰ 12.30-2.30pm & 7-10.30pm Mon-Sat; 🚊 San Stae; V

When plates of pasta seem too much and *cicheti* (Venetian tapas) too little, La Zucca is just right. Vegetablecentric Mediterranean small plates (€5 to €8) bring spice-trade influences to bear on local produce: zucchini comes with a ginger zing, carrots get curried

Spice up your life with a meal at Osteria La Zucca (p105)

with yoghurt, and rice pudding goes down easily with strawberries. Vegetarians can placate carnivorous travelling companions with roast lamb options, but veggies have the star quality here.

🍴 OSTERIA MOCENIGO
Cicheti, Classic Venetian €€
☎ 041 5231703; Salizzada San Stae; 🕑 noon-2.30pm & 7-10pm Tue-Sun; 🚊 San Stae
Times and dining habits have changed since dogi strained waistcoat buttons across the street at the Palazzo Mocenigo, where philosopher Giordano Bruno was turned in for heresy by his politically minded hosts. Here

you can make light meals of *cicheti* at the bar, or sit down to a casually elegant meal of roast razor clams, grilled fish and homemade pasta – and wax philosophical over Veneto wine by the glass.

🍴 VECIO FRITOLIN
Inventive Venetian, Sustainable Eating €€€
☎ 041 5222881; www.veciofritolin.it; Calle della Regina 2262; 🕑 noon-2.30pm & 7-10.30pm Tue-Sun; 🚊 San Stae
Peer past all the Slow Food awards plastered on the windows, and you'll spot a sign of the delicious food to come: blissed-out Italian foodies footing substantial lunch bills without flinching. Recent

standouts include homemade pasta with lagoon clams and wild hops; scallops roasted in their shells and dusted with truffle salt; and oven-baked lamb chops with sweet onions and roast potatoes. But since all the produce is hand picked daily at the Rialto markets – it's never canned or frozen – trust your savvy server to know what's best today. Gourmets on the go call ahead for the €10 fried-fish takeaway.

Y DRINK

Y AL PROSECCO *Wine Bar*
☎ 041 5240222; Campo San Giacomo dell'Orio 1503; ⏰ 9am-9pm Mon-Sat; 🚊 Riva di Biasio

Head to this bar for delightful prosecco without the pretence in a hidden gem of a *campo*. Sample a range of prosecco and other Veneto wines by the glass under a sun umbrella or with the locals at the bar, then when the bubbles ascend and protein seems advisable, order a platter of mixed cured meats or local cheeses. They're large enough to share, and this is the kind of congenial place where you might invite others to help you finish without it seeming the least bit odd.

Y LA RIVETTA *Pub*
Calle Sechera 637a; ⏰ 9am-9.30pm Mon-Sat; 🚊 Ferrovia

Cabernet franc comes out of a hose and platters of hearty fare are passed around at this favourite *bacaro* (bar) of salty sailors and neighbourhood eccentrics. Go for mixed plates with thick slabs of salami, translucent sheets of pancetta and grilled veggies with crusty bread. You can sit canalside, or head inside to admire the decor of bicycle parts and dusty bottles of English gin that were drained before the war. Buy a round to bring down the house.

★ PLAY

★ CASA DEL CINEMA *Cinema*
☎ 041 5241320; www.comune.venezia .it; Palazzo Mocenigo 1990; adult/student €6/5; ⏰ 9am-1pm & 3pm until shows end Mon-Fri, 3pm until shows end Sat; 🚊 San Stae

Between Venice Film Festivals, this film archive has become Venice's favourite venue for art-house films, Monday classic revivals and Wednesday-night events with film-makers. Fridays and Saturdays, indie film buffs carry debates across the street to Osteria Mocenigo (opposite) – but when family-friendly movies are screened on weekdays, kids race from here directly to Gelateria San Stae (p105). The centre is housed in Palazzo Mocenigo, the next entryway towards the canal from the Palazzo Mocenigo costume museum (p102).

>DORSODURO

In other cities, arty neighbourhoods are gritty, marginal districts that are best appreciated by grunge bands and collage artists. But Dorsoduro claims the very heart of the city and, instead of gloomy backstreet galleries, it has palatial buildings along the Grand Canal: Ca' Rezzonico, the Peggy Guggenheim Collection and the Gallerie dell'Accademia. There's far more glam than grit here, even in unlikely places. Paolo Veronese lavished his tiny neighbourhood church with masterpieces; Giambattista Tiepolo and Baldassare Longhena worked wonders on a convent that doubled as a hostel; and minimalist maestro Tadao Ando spent two years completing the Punta della Dogana's transformation from warehouse dock to contemporary-art showcase. But, somehow, this lavish attention hasn't gone to Dorsoduro's head. The neighbourhood still convenes nightly in Campo Santa Margherita for happy hour, queues up along the Zattere for gelato on sunny days, and haggles over the price of tomatoes at the produce barge alongside Campo San Barnaba.

DORSODURO

Please see over for map

◉ SEE

◉ CA' REZZONICO

☎ 041 2410100; www.museicivicivene
ziani.it; Fondamenta Rezzonico 3136;
adult/EU 6-14yr, student & senior €7/5,
free with Museum Pass; ⏲ 9am-1pm &
3pm until shows end Mon-Fri, 3pm until
shows end Sat; 🚊 San Stae

Other museums may illuminate, but
this one sparkles. This Longhena
palace showcases 18th-century arts
in music salons, boudoirs and even
a pharmacy complete with medici-
nal scorpions. Several salons are
crowned with ceilings by Tiepolo,
who literally goes over the top with
his sensuous beauty and shameless
flattery. His Throne Room ceiling
is a glimpse of heaven at the moment gorgeous Merit ascends to
the Temple of Glory, clutching the
Libro d'Oro (Golden Book), which
contained the names of Venetian
nobles – including the Rezzonico
family. Other highlights include
Pietro Longhi's socialite satires,
Guercino's dashing *Philosopher*
and Emma Ciardi's pointillist canal
views. Ask about classical music
concerts and other events held in
the ballroom. See p22 for more.

◉ CHIESA DI SAN SEBASTIAN

☎ 041 5282487; Campo San Sebastian;
adult/under 10yr €3/free, with Chorus
pass free; ⏲ 10am-5pm Mon-Sat;
🚊 San Basilio

Only in Venice could a modest
neighbourhood church be covered
with floor-to-ceiling Veronese
masterpieces. Veronese's horses
rear over the frames of the coffered
ceiling, his angels literally come
out of the woodwork and even
the organ doors are covered inside
and out with vivid Veronese works.
The only thing more colourful
than his brushwork is the popular
legend that claims Veronese found
sanctuary here in 1555 when he
fled murder accusations in Verona;
as a result, he couldn't do enough
to thank the parish. This story casts
a different light on Veronese's *Mar-
tyrdom of St Sebastian,* where the
bound saint defiantly stares down
his tormentors amid a local crowd
of fashionable nobles, turbaned
traders and, for comic relief, a frisky
lapdog.

◉ CHIESA DI SANTA MARIA DELLA SALUTE

☎ 041 5225558; Campo della Salute;
church free, sacristy €1.50; ⏲ 9am-noon
& 5-5.30pm; 🚊 Salute

Survivors of Venice's 1630 plague
built Our Lady of Salvation atop
at least 100,000 pylons as a
monumental gesture of thanks,
and Venetians still pray for health
here at least once a year (p30).
Architectural scholars have
noticed the similarity between
Longhena's unusual octagonal
design, and both Graeco-Roman

Angels in the architecture: gaze at Veronese's heavenly pictures in the Chiesa di San Sebastian (p109)

temples and Jewish cabbala diagrams; after the horrors of the plague, covering multiple religious traditions must have seemed like a wise health-insurance policy. The sacristy here holds Tintoretto's surprisingly up-beat *Wedding Feast of Cana,* plus no fewer than 12 Titians (see p16), including *St Marco Enthroned* (his earliest known work, from 1510) and a later *St Matthew* that's actually a self-portrait.

GALLERIE DELL'ACCADEMIA

☎ 041 5222247, bookings 041 5200345; www.gallerieaccademia.org; Campo della Carità 1050; adult/EU 18-25yr/under 18yr & senior €7.50/4.25/1; ⏱ 8.15am-2pm Mon, 8.15am-7.15pm Tue-Sun, ticket office closes 45min earlier; 🚢 Accademia

A multiplicity of masterpieces await behind the serene walls of this former convent. All the superstars of Venetian art are well represented here: Titian's red-hot sensuality, Tintoretto's action-packed drama, Vittore Carpaccio's gore-fests, Giovanni Bellini's Holy Family bonding moments, Rosalba Carriera's un-Botoxed portraits and Veronese's censored social commentary. Galleries are loosely organised by painter and time period; you'll have to pace yourself so you're not tempted to rush past

Rooms 16 to 18, which are packed with remarkable portraits, Canaletto's sweeping views of Venice and Giorgione's 1508 *La Tempesta*, an expressionist composition of blues and greens that was centuries ahead of its time.

GESUATI

☎ 041 5230625; Zattere 918; adult/under 10yr €3/free, with Chorus pass free; 🕙 10am-5pm Mon-Sat; 🚢 Zattere

If you're not yet sold on baroque art, just look up. On ceiling panels completed between 1737 and 1739, Tiepolo uses convincing architectural perspectives and heavenly colours that seem to lift the roof right off the place to tell stories from the life of St Dominic. On the right side of the nave is the 1730–33 *Saints Peter and Thomas with Pope Pius V* by fellow Venetian virtuoso of luminosity Sebastiano Ricci; it's quite a contrast to Tintoretto's adjacent 1565 *Crucifixion*, which glowers darkly in deep reds and greens. In this church, Venetian baroque puts the city's dark plague days in the past, ushering the sunny Zattere indoors instead.

PEGGY GUGGENHEIM COLLECTION

☎ 041 2405411; www.guggenheim -venice.it; Palazzo Venier dei Leoni, Fondamenta Venier dei Leone 701; adult/senior/student under 26yr/under 10yr

€12/10/7/free; 🕙 10am-6pm Wed-Mon; 🚢 Accademia

The possessor of a fortune after she lost her father on the *Titanic*, Peggy Guggenheim befriended dadaists and dodged Nazis while amassing avant-garde works by 200 modern artists. Peggy's palatial home is a now a modernist shrine highlighting Italian futurism, surrealist painting, and key works by ground-breaking expressionists Wassily Kandinsky, her ex-husband Max Ernst and Jackson Pollock (one of Peggy's many rumoured lovers). Since Peggy didn't collect for prestige, her art collection also features wonderful folk art and lesser-known artists, plus comparatively minor works by Pablo Picasso, Piet Mondrian and Salvador Dalí. Rather than following a favourite medium or trend, Peggy collected according to her own modernist ideals, and her sensibilities can be glimpsed throughout these galleries.

PONTE DELL'ACCADEMIA

🚢 Accademia

The steep wooden hump over the Grand Canal has put Accademia-bound tourists through their paces since 1933. The timber structure was meant to be a temporary replacement for a 19th-century metal bridge, but renovations are only now being undertaken – and the city reassures the bridge's

TREASURE HUNTS

You might not be able to find St Mark's missing kneecap inside the Basilica di San Marco or the Bellini that was whisked off the walls at Madonna dell'Orto in 1993, but other treasures await discovery in Venice.

Sunny summer weekends bring the *mercato delle pulci* (flea market) to the Campo Santa Margherita, along with the occasional Médecins Sans Frontières jumble sale, organised by two charming Venetian brothers who decided that retirement is boring, and the world needs all the help it can get. At these markets you'll spot antique Murano stemware, tiny copper pots in which you could cook *cicheti* (Venetian tapas) for dolls, and vintage Italian fashion magazines that have been hoarded in Venetian attics for decades.

Bochaleri in Giardini (Map pp60-1; www.bochaleri.it; Biennale gardens, Castello; 9am-5pm last weekends of month Apr-Nov; Biennale) is Venice's open-air show-case for local ceramic artisans, whose styles range from classic Renaissance portrait plates to sculptural *raku* (Japanese wood-fired pottery).

Mercantino dei Miracoli (9am-1pm & 3.30-7.30pm 1st weekend of month Mar-Dec; Ca' d'Oro) brings 1940s Murano glass buttons, 1800s silver tea services and other *palazzo* attic treasures at spring-cleaning prices to Campo Santa Maria Nova (Map pp72–3, G6), while **Mercantino dell'Antiquario** (Map pp42–3, C5; 333 9659994; www.mercantino camposanmaurizio.it; Campo San Maurizio; 9am-5pm last weekend Mar, Jun, Sep & Dec; Santa Maria del Giglio) sells antique ceramics, estate jewellery and tempestuous seascapes at prices that approach those of Sotheby's. Still, the scene is more sociable than an auction house – and where else are you going to find a used gondola prow, only slightly dented?

ardent admirers that changes are merely structural.

PUNTA DELLA DOGANA

199 139139; palazzograssi.it; Punta della Dogana; adult/student 12-25yr & senior/under 12yr & disabled €15/10/free, combined ticket with Palazzo Grassi €20/14/free; 10am-7pm Wed-Mon, last admission 1hr before closing; Salute

Fortuna – the weather vane atop Punta della Dogana – swung Venice's way when bureaucratic hassles in Paris convinced billion-aire contemporary art collector François Pinault to install his larg-est works in Venice's vacant 17th-century customs warehouses. Architect Tadao Ando flooded the halls with indirect light through polished-concrete channels and repurposed water gates – an elegant homage to Venetian modernist Carlo Scarpa's Biennale pavilion designs (p59).

SCUOLA GRANDE DEI CARMINI

041 5289420; Campo Santa Margherita 2617; adult/student €5/4;

⏱ **9am-6pm Mon-Sat & 9am-4pm Sun Apr-Oct, 9am-4pm daily Nov-Mar;**
🚤 **Ca' Rezzonico**

Eighteenth-century backpackers must have thought they'd died and gone to heaven at the Scuola Grande dei Carmini – up the most gorgeous staircase in Venice, to the right past Tiepolo's nine-panel ceiling of a resplendent *Virgin in Glory*, and through heavy doors was the lavish boiserie (carved timber) hostel where Carmelite nuns sheltered wayfarers. Cots are, sadly, no longer available in this jewel-box building, but the **Venice Opera** (www.venice-opera.com) sometimes stages performances here.

🔘 SQUERO DI SAN TROVASO

Campo San Trovaso 1097; 🚤 **Zattere**
When it's time for a tune up, gondolieri head to the *squero* (gondola workshop). The wood cabin on the corner of the Rio di San Trovaso may look like a misplaced ski chalet, but it's actually part of one of the city's three working *squeri*. Leave a tip in the jar to take a photo inside, but be sure not to disturb gondola-builders with sharp tools in hand.

🛍 SHOP

🔲 ANTICHITÀ TERESA BALLARIN *Antiques*

☎ **041 2771807; Calle delle Botteghe 3184;** ⏱ **4-7pm Mon, 10am-1pm & 3-7pm Tue-Sat;** 🚤 **Ca' Rezzonico**

Fabulous finds in styles ranging from rococo to rock and roll prove Venice's fashion heyday didn't end with baroque. Antique vases and paintings make fitting souvenirs, but 20th-century pieces are the real scores: futurist Bakelite rings, the odd Scarpa lamp, a rare ceramic vase by Gio Ponti and an op-art ladybird brooch, all for about what you'd pay for derivative works by modern designers.

🔲 AQUA ALTRA
Gifts, Sustainable Shopping

☎ **041 5211259; www.aquaaltra.it; Campo Santa Margherita 2898;** ⏱ **4-7.30pm Mon, 9.30am-12.30pm & 4-7.30pm Tue-Sat;** 🚤 **Ca' Rezzonico**
Venice has learned a thing or two about trading nicely with others since the days when it controlled maritime trade – hence this fair-trade boutique. Italian taste is matched with global conscience in single-origin chocolate from Sierra Leone cooperatives, footballs made by a Pakistani cooperative and handbags made from billboards hung on Venetian *palazzi*.

🔲 DANGHYRA *Ceramics*

☎ **041 5224195; www.danghyra.com; Calle delle Botteghe 3220;** ⏱ **10am-1pm & 3-7pm Tue-Sun;** 🚤 **San Tomà**
Architect Carlo Scarpa's spare shapes meet exuberant Venetian colour in ultramodern ceramics

Sigfrido Cipolato
Master goldsmith and jewellery artisan (p 66)

From sailor to jeweller I began studying ancient techniques – lost wax, micro-fusion – at port when I was in the navy in the 1960s. In the 1200s, apprentices were chosen by age six, and jewellers rarely selected their own sons; only those with exceptional promise were chosen. **Bejewelled skulls** The skull is a recurring motif in my jewellery – it's a *memento mori,* a reminder that life is short. During Rome's Inquisition, this was a moral lesson: think of the afterlife. But in Venice, it had the opposite meaning: live well while you can. **Shared pleasures** There's an element of risk working with precious materials: when you make a mistake in gold, you don't make the same mistake twice. But when it's exquisitely crafted, a treasure gives pleasure to the maker, the wearer, everyone who sees it. It's like poetry, or civility: they give life grace. **Handmade world** I live on the Lido, with its roads lined with pines and villas, but I work in the backstreets of Venice, as artisans do. Venice is not like the industrial world. Here people still make things with their hands, and you can find wonders if you seek them out. It's like chasing butterflies.

hand-thrown in Venice. Matte orange vases usher summer into any room, while gold crackle-glaze bowls make humble pasta dishes appear fit for a doge.

⌂ GUALTI *Jewellery*
☎ 041 5201731; www.gualti.it; Rio Terà Canal 3111; 🕙 10am-1pm & 3-7.30pm Mon-Sat; 🚉 Ca' Rezzonico

Either a shooting star just landed on your shoulder, or you've been to Gualti. Iridescent orange glass bursts from clear resin stems on an interstellar brooch, while metallic pink fused Lucite cascades from an invisible collar like fireworks. Like light displays on the lagoon, these movable pieces stir the imagination. Gualti doesn't like to repeat himself, but his prices (starting at €70) are less than you'd expect for one-off designs.

⌂ IL PAVONE *Paper Crafts*
☎ 041 5234517; Calle della Chiesa 721; 🕙 10am-1pm & 2.30-6pm Tue-Sat; 🚉 Accademia

Your *baccalà mantecato* (mashed cod prepared in garlic and parsley) is bound to come out better when the recipe is captured in a handmade book stamped with Gothic architectural patterns. Il Pavone's recipe books, travel journals and day planners are printed with traces of metallic pigments, but don't just judge them by their

shimmering covers. Inside, the books are well organised, with tabs for meal planning, headings to track your favourite sights and spots to note upcoming birthdays.

⌂ ELITRE *Fashion, Gifts*
☎ 041 0990067; Calle Crosera 3949; 🕙 10am-7.30pm Mon-Sat; 🚉 San Tomà

Extraterrestrial models stomp across the flat-screen TV, besotted garden gnomes radiate hearts on Fiorucci's Love Therapy T-shirts, and best friends square off over the last pair of purple polka-dotted Agatha Ruiz de la Prada Mary Janes only to re-bond over Hello Kitty housewares: it's just another day in the sale section at Elitre, Venice's trend store.

⌂ MADERA *Gifts, Homewares*
☎ 041 5224181; www.maderavenezia .it; Campo San Barnaba 2762; 🕙 4-7.30pm Tue-Sat; 🚉 Ca' Rezzonico

Frying pans look like clocks, spoons become tongues, and wooden salad bowls curl into waves: at Madera, household objects are transformed by elemental materials and organic shapes. Most pieces are by owner-designer Francesca Meratti and other Italian designers, with some Scandinavian and Japanese influences; prices start below €70 for steel-and-pearl rings and free-form wooden spoons.

SESTIERI

DORSODURO

🔲 MARINA E SUSANNA SENT
Glass, Jewellery
☎ 041 5208136; www.marinae
susannasent.com; Campo San Vio 669;
🕐 10am-1pm & 3-6.30pm Tue-Sat,
3-6.30pm Mon; 🚶 Accademia

Megaphones are no longer necessary to stand out in a crowd, thanks
to this whip-smart statement
jewellery by pioneering Murano
glass jewellery designers Marina
and Susanna Sent. Museum shops
throughout Venice feature the
sisters' signature 'soap' necklaces:
large, clear bubbles of thin yet
surprisingly sturdy glass that bring
a sense of humour to boardrooms
and first dates. Glass is paired with
unexpected materials in dramatic
teal-paper necklaces with oversized
purple-glass centrepieces, while an
organic double strand of tiny black-
and-white shells is emphatically
interrupted by a glossy lipstick-red
glass pendant.

🔲 PASTOR *Woodcarving*
☎ 041 5225699; www.forcole.com;
Fondamenta Soranzo della Fornace 341;
🕐 8.30am-12.30pm & 2.30-6pm Mon-
Sat; 🚶 Salute

The *forcola* (forked tongue of wood
where the gondola oar rests) for a
gondola is hand carved from acacia
and hard oak, and each *forcola*
must hold up under pressure and
express the style of its owner.
Sounds like a job for Saverio Pastor,

Blooming marvellous: Dorsoduro's flower stalls

who makes *forcole* that twist without losing their elegant balance
– just like the most experienced
gondolieri. Mick Jagger had his
forcola made to measure here, but
you can buy ready-made smaller
forcole to display as sculpture.

🍴 EAT

🍴 ANTICA PASTICCERIA TONOLO *Pastries*
€
☎ 041 5327209; Calle dei Preti 3764;
🕐 8am-8pm Mon-Sat, 8am-1pm Sun;
🚶 Ca' Rezzonico

Dire B&B breakfasts with packaged
croissants are corrected at Tonolo,
which serves flaky apple strudel
and oozing chocolate croissants.

Tide yourself through an early-evening concert with espresso and chocolate-topped beignets, their hazelnut-mousse filling as rich as a Venetian doge at tax-time.

DA NICO Gelato €
☎ 041 5225293; Zattere 922; ⏰ 7am-10pm Fri-Wed; 🚊 Zattere

Those sunny days when you're feeling too lazy for a trip to the Lido are perfect for Da Nico's dock. Pounce on free seats and order one of the house specialities: the *gianduiotto* (a slab of hazelnut gelato submerged under whipped cream) or *panna in ghiaccio* (frozen whipped cream sandwiched between cookies). Those specialities are half the price if you eat at the bar, but you'll want that seat once the gelato coma sets in.

ENOTECA AI ARTISTI
Italian €€
☎ 041 5238944; www.enotecaartisti.com; Fondamenta de la Toletta 1169a; ⏰ noon-4pm & 6.30-10pm Mon-Sat; 🚊 Accademia

The heart-warming pastas, seasonal bruschette and inspired cheese selections here can be paired, course by course, with wines by the glass suggested by your oenophile hosts. The glassed-in storefront makes for great people-watching, but space is limited so book ahead for groups larger than two.

GROM Gelato €
☎ 041 0991751; www.grom.it; Campo San Barnaba 2461; ⏰ noon-11pm; 🚊 Ca' Rezzonico

Take your tongue on a gelato victory lap of Italy, with flavours made from toasted Langhe hazelnuts, potent Sicilian strawberries and Amalfi lemons that permanently skew citrus standards. Several flavours are Slow Food– or Fair Trade–certified, and Grom uses real Marsala and organic free-range eggs for dreamy zabaglione.

IMPRONTACAFÉ
Italian, Sandwiches €€
☎ 041 2750386; Calle Crosera 3815; ⏰ 11am-11pm Mon-Sat; 🚊 San Tomà

Polenta, prosecco and espresso are the order of the hour, on the hour, for guests who come for lunch and stay through to evening. The best deals here are the mixed-plate combos, especially the grilled polenta with wild mushrooms, Venetian *sopressa* (salami) and salad. Architectural diagrams of cooking pots on blackboards and a Buddha presiding over the bar add a sly sense of humour to the sleek modern decor.

LA PROFETA Pizza €€
☎ 041 5237466; Calle Lunga San Barnaba 2471; ⏰ noon-3.30pm & 7-11pm Fri-Wed; 🚊 Ca' Rezzonico

Switch up your Venetian seafood diet with respectable pizza, grilled meats and duck *bigoli* (Venetian whole-wheat pasta) at this hide-away near Campo Santa Margherita. Garden seating is popular and service often overstretched; arrive early and not terribly famished.

PIZZA AL VOLO *Pizza* €
☎ 041 5225430; Campo Santa Margherita 2944; noon-1am;
Ca' Rezzonico
Peckish night owls fast run out of options in Venice after the *cicheti* (Venetian tapas) has gone and the restaurant kitchens have closed – but Pizza Al Volo has you covered. Slices here are cheap and respectable; they don't have a lot of fancy toppings, but they possess a thin yet sturdy crust that won't collapse on your going-out outfit.

RISTORANTE CANTINONE STORICO *Classic Venetian* €€€
☎ 041 5239577; Fondamenta di Ca' Bragadin 660-661; noon-3pm & 7-10pm Mon-Sat, closed Nov & Jan;
Accademia
The canalside seating here is nice, but don't hold out for it – and, once your pasta arrives, it'll command your attention anyway. Tagliatelle with asparagus, prawns and artichokes in *busura* (prawn sauce) may sound simple, but try telling

your taste buds. The restaurant's on the expensive side, but it's close to the Gallerie dell'Accademia and serves proper Venetian dishes without cutting corners.

RISTORANTE LA BITTA
Italian €€€
☎ 041 5230531; Calle Lunga San Barnaba 2753a; 7-10pm Mon-Sat;
Ca' Rezzonico
The daily bill of fare is presented on a miniature artist's easel, which is fair enough: the short, stout seasonal menu is a thing of beauty for anyone craving a nonseafood dinner. The *radicchio sformata* (savoury rocket pudding) is gooey with taleggio cheese, the pumpkin gnocchi are as rich as the Rezzoni-cos, and pork tenderloin in bacon-prune reduction is juicy enough to make you tuck in that napkin. The restaurant doesn't offer wine by the glass, but the staff will cut you a deal on a half bottle.

RISTORANTE SAN TROVASO
Classic Venetian €€
☎ 041 5230835; www.tavernasantrovaso.it; Calle della Accademia 967; noon-3.30pm & 7-11pm Fri-Wed;
Accademia
After the Accademia leaves you weak-kneed with beauty, you'll need a sit-down with fried calamari, polenta, *sarde in saor* (sardines in an onion marinade)

CLASS ACTS

Learn the local lingo, whip up a Venetian signature dish, row like gondolieri or go incognito in a self-made mask with the following courses.

Devise your own disguise for Carnevale – or for back at the office when the boss is looking for you – at **Ca' Macana** (☎ 041 2776142; www.camacana.com; Calle delle Botteghe 3172; class about €60; ⏰ 11am Mon, 2.30pm Fri; 🚊 Ca' Rezzonico). Two-and-a-half-hour courses on mask making and mask decorating are held in English in this backstreet artisanal mask-making studio; the bigger the group, the less it costs per head.

Get to know Venice inside out with English-language courses offered through the **Venetian Club** (☎ 345 8306533; www.thevenetianclub.co.uk), a community group of Venetians by birth and inclination working together to promote and advance Venice's cultural heritage. Classes include Venetian-style rowing, standing up on handcrafted boats (see p143); Venetian glass mosaics and glass jewellery; singing lessons to discover your inner La Fenice diva; traditional paper marbling and bookbinding; and a full-day culinary adventure, from shopping the Rialto markets to cooking a proper feast in a Venetian home.

At **Istituto Venezia** (☎ 041 5224331; www.istitutovenezia.com; Campo Santa Margherita 3116a; course per week €160-540; 🚊 Ca' Rezzonico) you can learn Italian by day in Campo Santa Margherita, then join the happy-hour small talk afterwards. Class prices vary according to class size, intensiveness and duration. To be the star pupil, consider one-on-one tutoring (charged by the hour).

and a carafe of the house soave before you'll begin to feel your toes again. Just around the corner from the museum, this sensibly priced rustic restaurant hastens your recovery, with brisk service, sunny garden seating and an airy, pleasingly simple wood-beamed dining room.

🍴 RISTOTECA ONIGA
Classic Venetian   €€

☎ 041 5224410; www.oniga.it; Campo San Barnaba 2852; ⏰ noon-3pm & 7-10pm Wed-Mon; 🚊 Ca' Rezzonico
Purists come for chef Annika's *nervetti* (calf's tendons) and Vene-

tian liver with onions, while gourmet rebels order the springtime-in-your-mouth ravioli with ricotta, broccoli and poppy seeds off the quirky seasonal menu. Either way you can't lose, and piazza seating and smooth service only sweeten the deal.

🍴 TRATTORIA DONA ONESTA
Classic Venetian   €

☎ 041 710586; www.donaonesta.com; Calle Dona Onesta 3922; ⏰ noon-3.30pm & 6.30-10pm; 🚊 San Tomà
At the Honest Woman tavern, devoted regulars are moved to truth over generous pours of house

SESTIERI

DORSODURO

Bottoms up at Cantinone 'Gia Schiavi'

wine, moaning about Berlusconi and raving about the vast bowls of mussels and clams: 'The owner's Egyptian, but he cooks like a Venetian.' Vegetarians will enjoy the veggie pasta with a roasted red-capsicum kick, and anyone pinched by euro exchange rates will appreciate the modest bill.

Y DRINK
Y CAFÉ NOIR *Cafe-Bar*
☎ 041 710925; Calle Crosera 3805;
🕑 7am-2am Mon-Fri, 5pm-2am Sat,
9am-2am Sun; 🚊 San Tomà
Morning espresso brings back the crowd that was here late last night, only a little the worse for

wear. Architecture students, musicians and travellers converge for *spritz* (prosecco-based cocktails) in the *calle* (street), so the quickest way to start a conversation is to state any of the following: Calatrava is overrated, Albinoni is underrated, and *spritz* with Aperol is better than *spritz* with Campari.

Y CAFFÈ ROSSO *Cafe-Bar*
☎ 041 5287998; Campo Santa Margherita 2963; 🕑 7am-1am Mon-Sat;
🚊 Ca' Rezzonico
The red heart of Campo Santa Margherita is this cafe, affectionately nicknamed Rosso after its red front window. Sunny mornings are well spent at a piazza table, commiserating over newspaper headlines with your neighbours then laughing it off with a prosecco at lunch. Evening brings the student crowd for a *spritz,* with entertainment provided by the cast of characters at the bar.

Y CANTINONE 'GIA SCHIAVI'
Pub, Wine Bar
☎ 041 5230034; Fondamenta Nani 992;
🕑 8.30am-8.30pm Mon-Sat;
🚊 Accademia
Good lungs and steady hands are essential to make your order heard over Cantinone's happy hour, and to transport your glass of wine or *pallottoline* (small bottle of beer) outside to the canal without spill-

ing it. Students, gondola builders and Accademia art historians all perch on canal railings and along the bridge, but remember: they've had more practice at not falling in than you.

☷ IMAGINA CAFÉ *Cafe-Bar*
☎ 041 2410625; www.imaginacafe.it; Rio Terà Canal 3126; ☽ 8am-2am Mon-Sat; ⚓ Ca' Rezzonico
Comfortable booths, works by emerging artists on the walls and a vast display of Aperol behind the bar all bring a creative, gay-friendly crowd that should prob-ably start paying rent here. Sunny piazza seating is usually thronged with locals and their little dogs, all of whom enjoy being admired.

☷ OSTERIA ALLA BIFORA
Wine Bar
☎ 041 5236119; Campo Santa Margherita 2930; ☽ 10am-2am; ⚓ Ca' Rezzonico
The staff aren't exactly quick with that Ferrari red meat slicer behind the bar, so just sip that wine, soak in the ambience of this roman-tic Romanesque bar, and don't count on your snacks to arrive any time soon. This place has a more mellow, enticing vibe than other places on the square, and

strangers have been known to get cosy at the communal tables.

☷ TEA ROOM BEATRICE
Tea House
☎ 041 7241042; www.bedandbreakfast -fujiyama.it; Calle Lunga San Barnaba 2727a; ☽ 10am-6pm; ⚓ Ca' Rezzonico
This tea house is an elegant alternative to bolting an espresso at a bar. Rainy days are good for iron pots of green tea and almond cake in the Japanese-themed tea room, while sunny days are for iced drinks and salty pistachios on the patio.

☆ PLAY
☆ VENICE JAZZ CLUB *Jazz*
☎ 041 5232056; www.venicejazzclub .com; Ponte dei Pugni 3102; admission incl drink €20; ☽ from 7pm Mon-Wed, Fri & Sat Sep-Jul; ⚓ Ca' Rezzonico
This place is suspiciously well organised for a jazz club, but the Venice Jazz Club Quartet keeps the vibe loose with improvisation-al tributes to jazz greats such as Miles Davis and Chet Baker. Drinks here are steep, so most locals start on the good stuff with the drink that comes free with admission, then backslide from there. Music starts at 9pm.

>GIUDECCA

Architecture binges have brought visitors to this corner of the lagoon for centuries, and no wonder – have you seen the Palladios? But this garden getaway for Venice's elite became the city's industrial outpost in the 19th century, resulting in an industrial sprawl of factories and apartment blocks. Giudecca earns street cred for being affordable and rough around the edges – and, like most city neighbourhoods that used to be industrial and iffy, it has recently become extremely cool. Defunct factories and waterfront warehouses have been converted to galleries, affordable lofts and a theatre, and although there's still a women's prison here, it's near a new luxe spa and a Harry's Bar offshoot. So, hop on the vaporetto (city ferry) to Giudecca now, while the air is electric with creative possibility and prices are still artist-friendly.

GIUDECCA

👁 SEE

🔘 CHIESA DI SAN GIORGIO MAGGIORE

☎ 041 5227827; Isola di San Giorgio Maggiore; church free, bell tower €3; 🕑 9.30am-12.30pm & 2.30-6.30pm Mon-Sat May-Sep, 9.30am-12.30pm & 2.30-4.30pm Mon-Sat Oct-Apr; 🔔 San Giorgio

Sunglasses become essential as you approach San Giorgio – this Andrea Palladio–designed masterpiece is set to dazzle. The white Istrian marble facade is almost blinding head-on, but close up you'll notice the depth of the massive columns that support

the tympanum, with the echoing triangles representing the Holy Trinity. This is possibly the only Venetian church where, once inside, you'll have to remind yourself to look at the paintings. Ceilings billow above, and high windows fill the space with filtered sunshine and easy grace. The black, white and red inlaid-stone floor will draw you towards the altar, which is flanked by two Tintoretto master-pieces: *Collecting the Manna* and *The Last Supper*. Sebastiano Ricci's sweet *Madonna Enthroned with Child and Saints* evokes an audible 'aww', as does the stirring pano-rama from atop the bell tower.

Grab those shades: Palladio's Chiesa di San Giorgio Maggiore is simply dazzling

PALLADIO: LOOKING GOOD AT 500

Before virtually every pillared bank and cupola-capped manor in the British Empire modelled itself on his designs, Andrea Palladio (1508–80) created churches and villas of surpassing lightness and strength in his native Veneto. Palladian facades across the Veneto were scrubbed until gleaming for the 500th anniversary of his birth in 2008, so now is the prime time to see his signature white marble edifices in all their near-blinding glory.

While romantics may be content to contemplate the gleaming facades of **Chiesa di San Giorgio Maggiore** (opposite) or **Il Redentore** (p128) from across the canal, architecture aficionados will want to get up close to appreciate the play of light and shade in multifaceted buildings, and step inside to see how vaulting, roof trusses and high windows create billowing, cloudlike ceilings. Once you're inside the buildings, John Ruskin's sniffy 19th-century denunciations of Palladio as a wannabe Roman architect seem hard to fathom. In these generous halls, the soaring uplift of Gothic architecture and the rational geometry of the Renaissance mingle seamlessly. Note the scrolled-paper capitals and the spare, clean surfaces; in them, you'll see precocious hints of rococo and even the historically minded high modernism of Le Corbusier and Tadao Ando.

◉ FONDAZIONE GIORGIO CINI

☎ 041 2710219; www.cini.it; Isola di San Giorgio Maggiore; guided monastery tours adult/student & senior €12/10, gallery admission varies; ۞ exhibitions 10am-6.30pm Mon-Sat, monastery tours 10am-4pm Sat & Sun; 🚊 San Giorgio

Before American heiresses and French billionaires got involved, culture in Venice was quietly being saved by Vittorio Cini. After escaping the Dachau concentration camp with his son Giorgio, he returned to Venice on a mission to save the Isola di San Giorgio Maggiore, which in 1949 was a ramshackle mess. His foundation bought and converted the island into a centre for arts and maritime culture, and converted a defunct nautical academy into a shipshape gallery space; recent exhibitions range from Sebastiano Ricci masterpieces to Peter Greenaway video projections. Tours of the ex-Benedictine monastery cover Palladio-designed cloisters and Longhena's grand staircase.

◉ GIUDECCA 795

☎ 340 8798327; www.giudecca795 .com; Fondamenta San Biagio 795; ۞ exhibitions 3.30-8pm Tue-Fri, 11am-8pm Sat & Sun; 🚊 Palanca

Do you follow the Titian colourists or do you go with the Tintoretto flow? Either way, Giudecca 795 has you in mind. It features contemporary artists with a strong sense of colour and dynamic line; look for Vito Campanelli's high-impact all-red paintings and Guitamachi's graphic train-track cityscapes.

📷 IL REDENTORE

☎ 041 5231415; Campo del Redentore 194; admission €3, with Chorus pass free; 🕙 10am-5pm Mon-Sat, 1-5pm Sun; 🚹 Redentore

The Black Death inspired this buoyant white church – started by Palladio in 1577 and finished by Antonio da Ponte in 1592 – which was commissioned in gratitude for the city's survival. There are some appealingly garish paintings by Gerolamo Bassano that look like black velvet, and a

characteristically stormy *Ascension* by Tintoretto and his school, but the most memorable work here is often overlooked: Paolo Piazza's 1619 *Gratitude of Venice for Liberation from the Plague*. Piazza shows the city held aloft by angels, using sombre grey tones and simple outlines to capture plague survivors' gratitude and guilt in a way that's strikingly modern.

🛍 SHOP

🛍 FORTUNY TESSUTI ARTISTICI *Homewares, Textiles*

☎ 041 5287697; www.fortuny.com; Fondamenta San Biagio 805; 🕙 9am-5pm Mon-Fri; 🚹 Palanca

At this design showroom, discover the subtly printed, elegantly draped silken fabrics that caused Marcel Proust to wax nostalgic. Fabrication methods have been jealously guarded for almost 100 years, and have yielded over 260 textile designs.

🍴 EAT

🍴 AI TRE SCALINI
Classic Venetian €€

☎ 041 5224790; Calle Michelangelo 53c; 🕙 noon-3pm Mon & Fri, noon-3pm & 7-10pm Tue, Wed, Sat & Sun; 🚹 Zitelle

Ouch. Belly laughs hurt after the generous plates of pasta and seafood here – not that that stops anyone. Families hold court on

Il Redentore: a white church for the Black Death

★ **Davide Amadio**
Interpreti Veneziani (p56) cellist with a rock-star following

Fish and art on Giudecca A couple of decades ago, Giudecca was mostly fishermen. Now you can find art shows, theatre, musicians – and still plenty of fish. **How baroque is like punk** Baroque composers experienced all the same emotions we do now – fear, passion, violence – back when people lived short, intense lives. We can play politely, or we can be true to the spirit of their work. **Jamming on a 1787 cello** This instrument was made for Venetian churches, with their perfect humidity and generous acoustics. When we travel, the wood dries and contracts, and I have to adjust how I play to get the right sound. **Soundtrack to Tintoretto** It's a tremendous privilege and challenge to play among Tintoretto's masterpieces at Scuola Grande di San Rocco [p86] – we're surrounded by giants. Because Tintoretto is so captivating, you have to work harder to bring people back to the present moment. But that's always true in Venice, right?

Looking for romance? Look no further than I Figli delle Stelle

weekends, friends converge for lunch in the garden, and wine flows straight from the barrel.

🍴 AL PONTIL DEA GIUDECCA
Classic Venetian €€
☎ 041 5286985; Calle Redentore 197a; 🕑 noon-3.30pm Mon-Fri; 🚮 Redentore
Asking for a menu here is like asking for one at your grandma's house. You'll have one of three daily specials and like it – really – and by the time lunch is over you'll feel like you should offer to help tidy up.

🍴 HARRY'S DOLCI
Inventive Venetian, Pastries €€€
☎ 041 5285777; www.cipriani.com; Fondamenta San Biagio 773;

🕑 10.30am-11pm Wed-Mon Apr-Oct; 🚮 Palanca
The service is low-key and the decor retro at this home away from home for the designer-sunglasses crowd, and though the prices have certainly kept up with inflation – think €15 for coffee and homemade *dolci* (dessert) – you could easily linger long enough to write whole novels. With views of the Zattere, and divine lemon tart served under the waterfront sun canopy, what's the rush?

🍴 I FIGLI DELLE STELLE
Inventive Venetian €€
☎ 041 5230004; www.ifiglidellestelle.it; Fondamente delle Zitelle 70;

⏱ 12.30-2.30pm & 7-11pm Tue-Sun;
🚊 Zitelle

Declarations of love at Venice's most romantic restaurant are slightly suspect – are you sure that's not the food talking? At I Figli delle Stelle, Luigi combines the velvety textures and heart-warming rustic fare of his native Puglia with the light touch and come-hither produce of Venice. A simple broad-bean cream soup with chicory and fresh tomatoes coats the tongue in a very naughty way, while ordering the mixed grill for two with langoustine, sole and fresh sardines hints that this could be serious (though many mains cost under €10). Book a waterfront table with San Marco views or canoodle on the leather couches inside.

⭐ PLAY

⭐ BAUER PALLADIO SPA *Spa*

☎ 041 5207022; www.palladiohotel
spa.com; Fondamenta della Croce 33;
🚊 Zitelle

When one too many grim airports has left you desperate for serenity, uplifting architecture and a serious scrub, head to this Palladio-designed former nunnery for a bath of milk, honey and rose petals (€90) with complimentary Jacuzzi and marble steam-room access.

⭐ TEATRO JUNGHANS
Theatre

☎ 041 2411974; www.teatrojung
hans.it; Campo Junghans 494b;
🚊 Redentore

Giudecca's ammunitions depot has been artfully repurposed as a cutting-edge theatre, where experimental performances end in explosive applause from select crowds of 150. Affectionately nicknamed Il Formaggino (The Cheese) for its triangular stage, Teatro Junghans is also the go-to venue for performance art between Biennales and theatrical workshops on costume design, mask-acting and *commedia dell'arte*.

>LIDO

Even the way it slides off the tongue in Italian sounds luxe and slightly louche: *Leeed*-oh. This 12km barrier island, which once housed the lagoon headquarters and quartered visiting navies, became hot property at the turn of the 20th century as a summer getaway from Venice's dark *calli* (streets) and stinky ebbing canals. Liberty villas and hotels sprung up around the island, the chic set moved in, and overnight the beaches became thronged with cabanas and large-hatted fashionistas. Lately the cabanas have been upgraded to four-poster day beds at beach party spots, and the Lido has increased its star power from solitary supernova Thomas Mann (who set *Death in Venice* here) to red-carpet constellations at the annual Venice Film Festival, held at the Palazzo del Cinema. The cars might come as a shock after a few days in traffic-free Venice, but the best way to get around is still biking – or strutting.

LIDO

◉ SEE
Antico Cimitero
  Israelitico **1** D1
Lido Beaches **2** C4
Palazzo del Cinema **3** B6

🍽 EAT
Da Tiziano **4** A6
Trattoria Andri **5** C4
Trattoria La Favorita **6** D2

🍸 DRINK
Colony Bar **7** C4

★ PLAY
Aurora Beach Club **8** D3
Lido on Bike **9** C3
Multisala Astra **10** C3

SANT'ELENA

Parco delle
Rimembranze

See Castello
Map pp60–1

Venice
International
University

Isola di
San Servolo

Laguna
Veneta

Isola di
San Lazzaro
degli Armeni
Mechitarist
Monastery

Isola del
Lazzaretto
Vecchio

To Ultima Spiagge
di Pachuka (1.5km)

San Nicolò

Antico
Cimitero
Israelitico

0   400 m
0   0.2 miles

Riviera San Nicolò

Via Morra
Via Marco Polo
Via F Morosini
Via F Duodo
Via Cipro
Via A Manzoni
Via Fasan
Via La Tito
Via Nicosia
Via Rovigno
Via C Gabola
Via F Negri
Via E Duodo
Via G
Via A Mauro
Via Dalmazia
Via S Gabato
Via C Zeno

Lido

Riviera S Maria Elisabetta

Piazzale S M
Elisabetta

Via Pisani
Via Lepanto
Via Sandro Gallo

Gran Viale Santa Maria Elisabetta

Via Corfu
Via P Paolo
Via Negroponte
Via Paolo Erizzo
Via Sgaravo
Via Zara
Via Loredan

Via Smime
Via Aquileia
Via Zeno

Lido di
Venezia

LIDO

Lungomare Gabriele d'Annunzio

Via Doge D Michiel
Via Enrico Dandola
Via Orso Partecipazio
Via Tron

Via G.B Grimani
Via Colombo
Via Spalato
Via Dardanelli

Via M.Bragadin

Via I Da Riva
Via J De
Cavalli
Via Jacopo Nani

Via Lemmo
Via Pisani
Via Sandro Gallo
Via Gallipoli
Via Lepanto

Hotel
des Bains

Via Morcelingo

Piazzale
Buccintoro

Lungomare Marconi

Via Lorenzo Marcello
Via Arduino
Via G Giovanni
Via A Barbaro
Via Quattro Fontane
Via Dardanelli

Via P Bembo
Via D Selvo
Via Rodi
Via V Fausti
Via Madonne
e Canone
Via Satrone

Via Catolla

Via F Morosini

Riva di Corinto
Via Sandro Gallo
Via A Emo

Via Lamberti
Via Buratti
Via Galupo

Piazza
Antonio

Piazza
Trau

Riva di Corinto

Via
Foscari
Piazza
Flume

Via Dalmazia

Via J De
Cavalli

Lido
Beaches

Golfo di
Venezia

Former
Casino

Piazzale
del Casino

Lungomare Marconi

To Malamocco (3km)

👁 SEE

👁 ANTICO CIMITERO ISRAELITICO

Ancient Jewish Cemetery; ☎ 041 715359; www.museoebraico.it; tour adult/student & Venice Card holders €8.50/7; ☺ guided tours 2.30pm Sun Apr-Sep by prior reservation; 🚊 San Nicolò

Epic poems seem to almost write themselves in this quiet, overgrown garden, which was Venice's main Jewish cemetery from 1386 until the 18th century. As a result, the tombstones range in design from Venetian Gothic to distinctly Ottoman. One-hour tours organised by the Museo Ebraico di Venezia (p74) provide an insight into the life and times of those buried here; English-language tours meet at the cemetery gate and are usually held on the last Sunday of the month.

👁 LIDO BEACHES

deposit/chair/umbrella & chair/hut €5/6/11/17; ☺ 9.30am-7pm May-Sep; 🚊 Lido

Beach chairs and bronzed lifeguards may seem a world apart from muggy, ripe Venice, but they're actually only a 15-minute ferry ride away. Most Lido beaches charge for chair, umbrella and hut rental, but after 2pm the tanning crowd thins out and rates drop a

Take some time out on a Lido beach

BEST. PARTY. EVER

Venice party planners outdid themselves for the reception of young King Henry III of France in 1574. As he approached the city on a royal barge rowed by 400 oarsmen, glass-blowers blew molten glass on rafts alongside the ship for his entertainment. (Sure beats balloon animals!) On arrival, the king was greeted by a bevy of Venetian beauties dressed in white and dripping family jewels into deep décolletages. Then came dinner: 1200 dishes, 300 bonbons and napkins made from spun sugar. But the masterstroke was the all-star decorations committee of Andrea Palladio, Paolo Veronese and Tintoretto, who built and painted triumphal arches for the occasion. Try topping that at your next office party.

couple of euros. To avoid amenities fees and throngs of Italian weekenders, rent a bike and head south to Alberoni, and other more pristine beaches.

🅖 MALAMOCCO
off Map p133; 🅛 **Lido**
If Venice got left in the dryer, it might come out as tiny canal-filled Malamocco, the lagoon capital from AD 742 to 811. Pass over Ponte di Borge to explore the *calle* of this less overwhelming lagoon town, which has just a handful of *campi* (squares), churches, *osterie* (restaurant-bars) and grand *palazzi* (palaces or mansions).

🅞 PALAZZO DEL CINEMA
🅛 **Lido**
This rigid airport-terminal structure seems as ill-suited to the playboy Lido as a woolly bathing suit – but the white walls make striking backdrops for red carpets and tanned stars at the Venice

Film Festival (p18). See the controversial venue while you can: this icon of Fascist architecture may be replaced by a multiplex.

🍴 EAT

🍴 **DA TIZIANO** *Cicheti, Pizza* €
☎ **041 5267291; Via Sandro Gallo 96;** 🕑 **noon-3pm & 7-10pm Tue-Sun;** 🅛 **Lido**
Keeping it real on the Lido, this local hangout serves respectable *cicheti* (Venetian tapas) and decent pizza at fair prices to a regular happy-hour crowd. If movie stars drop by, well, that can't be helped – after all, this is the handiest pizzeria to the Palazzo del Cinema.

🍴 TRATTORIA ANDRI
Classic Venetian €€€
☎ **041 5265482; Via Lepanto 21;** 🕑 **1.30-4pm Wed-Sun;** 🅛 **Lido**
While others tan midday away, foodies head for a leisurely lunch

BIKING THE LIDO

Stretch your legs and see more of the Lido on a bike, available by the hour or day at the self-evidently named **Lido on Bike** (☎ 041 5268019; www.lidoonbike.it; Gran Viale 21b; bike per hr single/tandem/double/family €3/6/8/15, bike per day single/tandem €10/18; ✆ 9am-7pm Mar-Oct; ⚓ Lido). This friendly bike-rental shop right near the Lido vaporetto (city-ferry) stop has reasonable prices and a map thrown in gratis. You must have official identification showing you're at least 18 to rent a bike.

Reserve a bike for the whole day so you don't have to rush – that'd defeat the whole point of laid-back Lido. For an easy loop that takes a couple of hours, start at the Lido vaporetto stop and head 3km south along the tree-lined, beachfront Lungomare Guglielmo Marconi to Malamocco (p135), where you can explore a miniature version of Venice. Mind the traffic – after a couple of days in pedestrian-only Venice, it's easy to forget the rules of the road. Then head back along Lungomare Guglielmo Marconi – braking for beauty, beaches and gelato like a local – and hang a left after the Palazzo del Cinema (p135) onto Via Quattro Fontane. Take a right along the canal onto Via S Giovanni d'Acri, which turns into winding Via Lepanto; make a pit stop for lunch at Trattoria Andri (p135), or take Gran Viale Santa Maria Elisabetta to Aurora Beach Club (opposite) to flop on a four-poster beach bed.

at this canalside restaurant. The menu at Trattoria Andri focuses on simply prepared seafood: shrimp salad, grilled fish and *fritto misto* (fried seafood). Wash it down with well-priced wines and homemade sorbets, then see if you can make it back to that beach chair.

🍴 TRATTORIA LA FAVORITA
Classic Venetian €€
☎ 041 5261626; Via Francesco Duodo 33; ✆ 6-10pm Tue, noon-3.30pm & 7.30-11pm Wed-Sun, closed Jan–mid-Feb; ⚓ Lido
Spider-crab gnochetti, fish risotto and mixed *crudi* (composed bites of raw fish), all at noncelebrity prices, make La Favorita live up to

its name. You should book ahead for the breezy, wisteria-filled garden – it's always a hot spot for visiting movie moguls and stubborn songbirds who aren't about to be outdone by all those mobile-phone rings.

🍸 DRINK

🍸 COLONY BAR *Lounge*
☎ 041 5265921; www.desbainsven ezia.com; Hotel des Bains, Lungomare Guglielmo Marconi 17; ✆ 9am-1am May-Oct; ⚓ Lido
Celeb-spotting and cocktails on a historic Liberty-style verandah that's elegantly secluded by maritime pines – ah, this is Lido living. Your drink tab will easily match

your cabana rental for the day, but you'll enjoy all the five-star perks – fawning service, top-shelf hooch, even lobby wi-fi access – without paying the Hotel des Bains room rate.

⭐ PLAY

⭐ AURORA BEACH CLUB
Beach Club, DJs

☎ 041 5268013; www.aurora.st; Lungomare Gabriele D'Annunzio 20x; 🕐 8.30am-2am May-Sep; 🚊 Lido

After a long day relaxing and unwinding on a lounger, there's nothing better than relaxing and unwinding on a carved four-poster beach bed. Days flow into nights at this venue, aided by diversions such as free books and magazines, beach-sport and chill-out zones, live-music sets, cocktail bars, an open-air cinema and DJ sets that will keep you on the dance floor until you face plant on the sofa.

⭐ MULTISALA ASTRA *Cinema*
☎ 041 5265736; Via Corfu 9; adult/ student & senior €7/5; 🕐 shows 5.30-10pm; 🚊 Lido

When you start feeling the burn on the beach, catch a show at this dark, air-conditioned cinema instead. The program is planned by the Venice municipal film commission, which makes sure there are art-house options alongside blockbusters.

⭐ ULTIMA SPIAGGIA DI PACHUKA *Beach Club, DJs*
off Map p133; ☎ 348 3968466; Viale V Klinger, Spiaggia San Nicolò; admission varies; 🕐 noon-10pm Sun-Thu, noon-2am Fri & Sat May-Sep; 🚊 San Nicolò

This place has all the sand of the Lido and all the laid-back boardwalk attitude of the Zattere, plus beer, pizza, and space for emerging artists among the beach umbrellas. Live music starts at 10pm on Fridays, with DJs working turntables on Saturdays and salsa dancing on Sundays.

>THE LAGOON

Other cities have suburban sprawl and malls – Venice has a teal blue lagoon dotted with photogenic islands and rare wildlife. Sometimes separated only by narrow channels, the city's outlying islands range from celebrated glass centres and a former Byzantine capital to deserted nunneries and garden isles. Serious shoppers hop the vaporetto (city ferry) to Murano, snapping up limited-edition glass pieces created with techniques that have been used since the 8th century; escapists prefer lazy days spent boating on the lagoon. Spot mohawked storks balancing thoughtfully on one leg and cormorants holding their wings out to dry after a fish dinner, then head to the fishing isle of Burano to get your own seafood meal amid a cheerful riot of colour-saturated houses. The golden mosaics at Torcello's Cattedrale di Santa Maria Assunta end lagoon adventures on a heavenly note.

Become enlightened on Murano (p141), where too much glass is never enough

SESTIERI

THE LAGOON

👁 SEE
BURANO

Map p140; 🚤 **Burano, Mazzorbo**

Strip away Venice's monumental overdose on Gothic ornamentation and crank up the colour palette from pastel to punchy, and there you have the charming island of Burano, located a 40-minute ferry ride from San Marco. Come for the colours, then stay for the cookies: Burano's vaguely lemony, crumbling ring- and S-shaped biscuits are ideal for dunking in dessert wines. Burano was traditionally famous for its lace, but at the time of writing the Museo di Merletto (Lace Museum) was closed for restoration and much of the lace for sale in Buranelli boutiques was imported; be sure to ask for a guarantee of authenticity if you're buying. When lace-crazed tour groups descend on the island, cross the wooden bridge to neighbouring Mazzorbo to find plenty of green space, a playground and a seemingly sacrilegious public toilet in the apse of a former chapel. See p24 for more on Burano.

VENICE BY BOAT

See Venice as Venetians have for centuries: by boat. Beyond brief jaunts on a gondola or a vaporetto (city ferry), the following boating outings offer maritime adventures on traditional Venetian boats. Reserve ahead, bring sunscreen and check weather forecasts, since these boat trips are subject to weather conditions.

> **Row, row, row your boat like gondolieri do** with Jane Caporal (p143) of **Row Venice** (☎ 345 2415266; www.rowvenice.com; 2hr lessons from €40). Leave your land-lubber days behind and find your footing on the sparkling lagoon, with Jane showing you how to propel her handcrafted Venetian *sandolo* (flat-bottomed boat) standing up, using a single oar. Glide past Venice's island cemetery, pause for a picnic (book ahead), and hop up on the *poppa* (stern) to learn to row while singing, gondolieri-style.

> **Sail away** with **Laguna Eco Adventures** (☎ 329 7226289; www.lagunaecoadventures.com; tour €40-120) in a Venetian *sampierota*, a twin-sailed boat small enough to slip into canals but sturdy enough to glide across open water. The boats accommodate five people maximum, so it's just you, seagulls, and the wind at your backs. Itineraries range from a circuit of outlying islands to an easy drift along the backstreets of Venice at sunset.

> **Reach the outer lagoon limits** with **Terra e Acqua** (☎ 347 4205004; www.terraeacqua.com; tour incl lunch €70-120). Skipper Cristina della Toffola leads trips for up to 10 people in her sturdy motorised *bragosso* (Venetian barge), calling at plague quarantine islands, fishing and bird-watching hotspots, Burano and Torcello. Cristina is a wealth of information on lagoon wildlife and island history, plus she serves a mean fish stew and *spritz* (prosecco-based cocktail) at picturesque mooring spots.

MURANO

Brick warehouses and industrial smokestacks disguise the combustible creativity held within Murano's glass studios and showrooms. Hear the eerie heavy breathing of furnaces along the *fondamente* (canal banks) and follow the red glow into studios to glimpse glass-blowing in progress. For shoppers, however, the main attraction of Murano is obvious: the showrooms, where prices for hand-blown original glass works are as good as they're going to get.

ⓒ MURANO COLLEZIONI

Map p142; ☎ 041 736272; www.muranocollezioni.com; Fondamenta Manin 1c-d; ⏰ 10am-5pm Tue-Sun; 🚉 **Colonna**

Like divas at La Fenice, the signature glass pieces in this darkened brick warehouse show perfect poise on their elegantly spotlighted pedestals. Famed Murano glass-designers Barovier&Toso,

MURANO

Carlo Moretti and Venini are all represented here, and even if you're not in the market for such high-end glass you're welcome to admire their luminous designs.

MUSEO DEL VETRO

Museum of Glass; Map p142; ☎ 041 739586; www.museiciviceneziani .it; 8 Fondamenta Giustinian; adult/EU 6-14yr, student & senior €6.50/4, with Museum Pass free; ⏱ 10am-6pm Thu-Tue Apr-Oct, 10am-5pm Thu-Tue Nov-Mar, ticket office closes 30min earlier; 🚊 Museo

Centuries ago, glass-blowers who left Murano risked assassination; since 1861, however, Murano has shared its secrets and major innovations at the Museo del Vetro. Roman glass from the 3rd century AD is featured alongside clever postmodern works, including Maria Grazia Rosin's 1992 spray bottle and detergent jug, both made from impeccably blown glass. Upstairs there's an explanation of how glass is made, including a discussion of the technique used to create Venetian trade

Jane Caporal
Perth-born Venetian rowing coach of Row Venice (p141)

From vacationer to Venetian When I first visited from Perth, some nice students offered to show us around Venice. The rest is your classic vacation romance – I moved to Venice 20 years ago, and my husband Luigi and I are raising our two sons here – only this one winds up in a rowboat. **Have no fear** Venetian rowing is done standing up, but since you push forward, you're more likely to fall inside the boat. Besides, Venetian waters are often only knee-deep. When people do fall in – usually when they've had an extra *spritz* (proseco-based cocktail) – they tell canal-slime stories for *years*. **Campionessa-in-training** It took four years to work up the courage, but that first time I rowed the Grand Canal was a big buzz. I wanted everyone to see how great it was, so I did my teacher training with CONI (Italy's Olympic institute). To be a *campionessa* (champion), you have to win a city race. Why not take the oar and try it?

beads. Across the hall are 17th-century baroque glass triumphs such as winged goblets, plus Carlo Scarpa's 1930 octopus and Romano Chirivi's 1968 *Inutili* (Useless) wineglasses, which require drinking straws.

TORCELLO

This wild island was once Ernest Hemingway's favourite hunting ground, but its true claim to fame is as a former capital of Byzantium. From the vaporetto stop it's a 10-minute stroll past lagoon ducks and sheep pens to the charmingly overgrown central piazza, which contains a small museum and antiques shop. But across this square is the real treasure: the Cattedrale di Santa Maria Assunta. See p24 for more on Torcello.

◉ CATTEDRALE DI SANTA MARIA ASSUNTA

Map p140; ☎ 041 296 0630; Piazza Torcello; church/bell tower/church & bell tower/church, bell tower & museum €4/4/7.50/10; ⏱ 10.30am-6pm Mar-Oct, 10am-5pm Nov-Feb, last entry 30min earlier; 🚇 Torcello

At this mesmerising medieval church, life choices are presented as a mosaic cautionary tale: look ahead to a golden afterlife with

Medieval visions of hell at the Cattedrale di Santa Maria Assunta

the beatific Madonna gleaming in the apse, or turn your back on her and face the blue devil gloating over skewered souls and skulls squirming with worms. If time permits, climb the bell tower (last entry one hour before closing time) for views of the lagoon, or browse Roman bronzes and stone relics from Torcello's Byzantine heyday at the quirky little museum across the piazza.

🛍 SHOP

MURANO

🛍 CAMPAGNOL & SALVADORE *Glass*

☎ 041 736772; Fondamenta San Giovanni dei Battuti 8; ☽ 10.30am-6pm Mon-Sat; 🚉 Colonna

A light touch is essential for the delicate art of Murano mouth-blown glass, but Campagnol & Salvadore's glass creations are light-hearted too. Their aqua-and-sunshine-yellow bead necklaces look like strands of tiny beach balls, and hypnotically swirled orange and burgundy cups appear to have been pulled from a magician's hat. Chic matte finishes and psychedelic, Tim Burton-esque colour schemes make these baubles runway-ready and circus-fabulous. Aspiring designers are encouraged to create their own looks from individual blown-glass beads (€3 to €15).

🛍 ELLEELLE *Glass*

Map p142; ☎ 041 5274866; www.elle ellemurano.com; Fondamenta Manin 52; ☽ 10am-6pm Mon-Sat; 🚉 Colonna

Unexpected asymmetrical shapes and striking two-colour combinations have been the trademark of these modernist masters since the 1950s; today Nason Moretti's third-generation glass designers are layering heavy crystal over coloured glass to create vases that look like pure liquid colour trapped in ice. Prices start at a surprisingly reasonable €31 for signed hand-blown drinking glasses, but with growing interest from museums in the US, don't expect the deals to last forever.

🛍 NEROPACO *Glass*

☎ 041 736801; Fondamenta Vetrai 58; ☽ 10am-6pm Mon-Sat; 🚉 Colonna

Either aliens have landed on your ceiling, or you've already paid a visit to Orovetro, designers of Murano modernist blown-glass chandeliers. From molten glass in dramatic colours – glossy black, pale gold or the signature Alexandrite lilac – these mood-lighting maestros create mesmerising lamps that seem to shape-shift from deep-sea creatures into intergalactic flowers. Neropaco's chandelier prices are among the best in Murano, and they'll ship that mod disc lamp anywhere.

Discover an eye for colour on picture-perfect Burano (p140)

🍴 EAT

BURANO

🍴 TRATTORIA AL GATTO NERO *Classic Venetian* €€€

Map p140; ☎ 041 730120; www
.gattonero.com; Via Giudecca 88;
🕑 noon-3.30pm & 7.30-9.30pm Tue-
Sun; 🚢 Burano

Italian foodies, movie stars and
dignitaries have taken such a
shine to this Burano restaurant that reservations are now
necessary in this out-of-the-way
spot. But once you've tried the
homemade tagliolini with spider
crab, risotto with langoustine,
ultrafresh grilled fish and perfect
house-baked Burano biscuits, a
phone call – or even a swim from
Venice – seems like a minor effort
to make for such a major meal.
This is a good place to opt for
canalside seating, because you
won't be neglected; meals are
served efficiently, with pleasant
banter in English and a proud
Buranesi flourish.

MURANO

🍴 BUSA ALLA TORRE *Classic Venetian* €€

☎ 041 739662; Campo Santo Stefano 3;
🕑 11.30am-3.30pm; 🚢 Faro

The €13 set menu draws crowds to
Murano's classic eatery – arrive early for tangy *sarde in saor* (marinated
sardines), plump prawn pasta and
piazza seating with tempting views
of glass showrooms.

TORCELLO

🍴 RISTORANTE AL TRONO DI ATTILA *Classic Venetian* €€

☎ 041 730094; www.altronodiattila.it;
Fondamenta Borgognoni 7a; 🕑 noon-
3.30pm daily Apr-Oct, noon-3.30pm
Tue-Sat Nov-Mar; 🚢 Torcello

Good cheer and honest prices
make for relaxing lunch breaks
along the footpath between
Torcello's vaporetto stop and
Cattedrale di Santa Maria Assunta.
Unwind under the pergola with
seafood risotto, house wine and
Torcello's bucolic soundtrack of
bleating sheep.

SESTIERI

THE LAGOON

Bliss is never more than a bridge and a couple of *calli* (streets) away in Venice, but here are a few pointers to get you there that much faster.

Gilberto Penzo (p88): a model boat builder

ACCOMMODATION

First things first: you do not have to stay on the mainland, missing the opportunity to wake up in fairy-tale Venice. Whoever keeps circulating the rumour that Venice doesn't have enough beds and offers no rooms under €200 is about a decade out of date – and hasn't heard of the internet.

Over the past 10 years, many Venetians have opened their homes as B&Bs or *affitacamere* (rooms for rent). These places are much more personable than Venice's big hotels, and they're often tucked away in neighbourhoods where you can mingle with the locals but still be close to the sights. Better still, you can compare costs online, then negotiate a rate that fits your budget by emailing the hotel or B&B directly. Compare hotels and inns at www.veneziasi.it; search B&B options at www.bbplanet.it; and find apartment vacation rentals and housing swap offers listed at http://venice.it.craigslist.it. The Azienda di Promozione Turistica (APT) lists more than 475 *affitacamere* and B&Bs plus 200 apartment rentals at www.turismovenezia.it. With research, you can find places that don't double their low-season price in high season, and even a few places under €100.

If you're still thinking of staying in Mestre, consider the following scenario. You stay in Venice until sundown to get the full effect of this romantic city, linger over a *spritz* (prosecco-based cocktail), then decide you'll try a promising Venetian *osteria* (restaurant-bar) you read about in this book (clever you). After a lovely meal, you have to catch a train to Mestre; even if your hotel is in a nice part of town, the train station certainly isn't. Tomorrow, instead of waking up to the sound of gondoliers crying 'Oooooeee!', you've got a symphony of honks at Mestre rush hour.

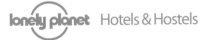 Hotels & Hostels

Need a place to stay? Find and book it at lonelyplanet.com. Over 50 properties are featured for Venice – each personally visited, thoroughly reviewed and happily recommended by a Lonely Planet author. From hostels to high-end hotels, we've hunted out the places that will bring you special experiences. Read independent reviews by authors and other travellers, and get practical information including amenities, maps and photos. Then reserve your room simply and securely via Hotels & Hostels – our online booking service. It's all at lonelyplanet.com/hotels.

So, that said: where would you like to stay in Venice? The most reasonably priced B&Bs and *affitacamere* are in residential sections of Santa Croce, San Polo and Cannaregio; B&Bs in San Marco, Dorsoduro and Castello tend to be pricier. Dorsoduro and San Marco offer many boutique accommodation optionss, Cannaregio is good for quiet and period charm, and Santa Croce and Giudecca offer a Venetian experience just off the tourist trail.

When nothing less than a *palazzo* (palace or mansion) with a Grand Canal view will do, try San Marco. Several of the historic palaces along the Grand Canal have been bought by hotel chains, adding an air of brisk efficiency to these luxury operations. The Starwood-run Gritti Palace has maintained its swagger and antique charm, while the Monaco & Grand Canal Hotel – a former high-baroque gambling den – has recently completed an elegant renovation. For a luxury waterfront stay, you might also consider staying in a Palladio-designed cloister at the new Bauer Palladio & Spa or head to the Lido for the Liberty art deco grandeur of the Hotel des Bains.

BEST SPLURGES
> Bauer Palladio (www.palladiohotel spa.com)
> Gritti Palace (www.starwood hotels.com)
> Palazzo Abadessa (www.abad essa.com)
> Hotel Palazzo Barbarigo (www .designhotels.com)
> Hotel Metropole (www.hotel metropole.com)

BEST DESIGNER B&BS
> Charming House DD.724 (www.the charminghouse.com)
> Palazzo Soderini (www.palazzo soderini.it)
> Domus Orsoni (Domus Orsoni)
> Bloom/7 Cielo (www.bloom -venice.com)
> Oltre Il Giardino (www.oltreil giardino-venezia.com)

BEST FOR PERIOD CHARM
> Hotel Flora (www.hotelflora.it)
> Pensione La Calcina (www.lacalcina .com)
> Locanda Barbarigo (www.locanda barbarigo.com)
> Hotels des Bains (www.desbains venezia.com)
> Locanda Cipriani (www.locanda cipriani.com)

BEST UNDER €100
> Pensione Guerrato (www.pensione guerrato.it)
> Foresteria Valdese (www.foresteria venezia.it)
> Hotel Ai Do Mori (www.hotelaido mori.com)
> Palazzo Zenobio (www.collegio armeno.com)
> Venice Resorts (www.venice resorts.it)

SNAPSHOTS

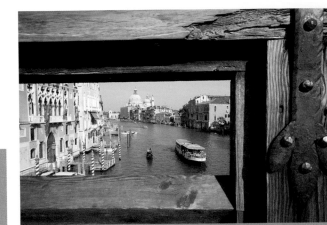

GRAND CANAL

How grand is it, really? With some 50 palaces, six churches, four bridges, scene-stealing cameos in four James Bond films, two open-air markets and one rather picturesque prison (from the outside, anyway), this water-way definitely earns its name and fame. To get the full effect, travel the length of the Grand Canal at night, when dock lights turn into frenzied Tintoretto brush strokes on the water, and Murano chandeliers and Tiepolo ceilings can be glimpsed through *palazzo* windows.

To max out on romance, tour the Grand Canal by *sampierota* (narrow sailboat) or gondola at night. During the day, *motoschiaffi* (motor boats) whiz past and kick up wakes that upset smaller crafts and wear away the *fondamente* (canal banks) of the Grand Canal, much to the dismay of Venetians in general, but especially of gondolieri, who can get grumpy when asked to take the Grand Canal. So unless you have a yacht and filming clearance – like Daniel Craig in *Casino Royale* – vaporetto (city ferry) 1 is your best bet to cover the Grand Canal by day. With a 12-hour vaporetto ticket, you can hop on and off wherever you like en route to San Marco. Embark at the train station, and as you chug up the canal, keep an eye out for the following landmarks.

On the right, the baroque Baldassare Longhena–designed Ca' Pesaro (p99) juts out into the canal. Housing a modern-art gallery and the Museo Orientale, this *palazzo* has a deep double arcade atop a faceted marble base, and chiselled good looks to rival any Bond.

The next vaporetto stop on your left is the Venetian Gothic Ca' d'Oro (p71), with two tiers of peekaboo quatrefoil portholes lightly balancing atop lacy arcades. Beauty queen that it is, the Ca' d'Oro is capped with crenulation that looks like a tiara. Hop off here to check out Andrea Mantegna's magnificent *St Sebastian* and other Napoleonic plunder.

In the morning, you'll hear the Rialto produce markets (p94) and covered Pescheria (p94) before you see them on your right. Fishmongers call out the catch of the day in Venetian dialect, and vendors brag shamelessly about their artichokes. If your stomach's growling, there's a vaporetto stop here. Otherwise, continue under the Ponte di Rialto (p86), watching tourists hanging off the side of the bridge like gargoyles to get the best photo.

As you round the next bend, the splendid Longhena-designed Ca' Rezzonico (p109) will be on your right, with two storeys of grand window arcades to shed natural light on the Tiepolo ceilings inside. Hop off at the vaporetto stop out front to binge on baroque art here.

Staring down the Ca' Rezzonico from across the canal is the Palazzo Grassi (p47), recently resuscitated by billionaire François Pinault with minimalist architect Tadao Ando. The front dock is a contemporary sculpture installation featuring floating conversation pieces such as Subodh Gupta's giant skull made of cooking pots. To see the Grassi's latest show, disembark at the next stop at the Ponte dell'Accademia (p113).

Keeping a low profile on the right bank is the Peggy Guggenheim Collection (p113). Look for the Alexander Calder by the dock, and peek between the shrubs for Marino Marini's 1948 *Angel of the City,* a nude figure on a horse who is very excited indeed by this view of the Grand Canal. For a closer look, get off at the next vaporetto stop in front of the Chiesa di Santa Maria della Salute (p109). This unusual octagonal shrine echoes Roman temples to Venus and mystical cabbala diagrams, and contains early Titians. Next door at Punta della Dogana (p114), Tadao Ando has converted Venice's customs warehouses into an eyebrow-raising contemporary art gallery.

End your Grand Canal tour near Piazza San Marco at the San Zaccaria stop, passing the Ducal Palace (p45) on your left and entering the Prigioni Nuove (New Prisons) just in time for your chamber music concert (p69).

Top left Take in the grand view from the Ponte dell'Accademia (p113)

FOOD

Local Food! may be the latest foodie motto, but it's nothing new in Venice. Surrounded by garden islands and a lagoon's worth of seafood, Venice offers local specialities that never make it to the mainland, because the produce is all served fresh the same day in Venetian *bacari* (bars) and *osterie*. But Venice's cosmopolitan outlook must also be credited with keeping the city ahead of the foodie curve. After making an art of traditional Venetian recipes like *sarde in saor* (sardines in an onion marinade) and *baccalà mantecato* (mashed cod prepared in garlic and parsley), Venetian cooks are reinventing them with spice-route flavours from Venice's trading past. The occasional exceptional ingredient from another part of Italy sneaks in, such as Tuscan beef fillets and Sicilian blood oranges – but only in moderation.

Luckily for you, there's still room at the bar to score the best *cicheti* (Venetian tapas), and reservations are still readily available for phenomenal eateries. Stories about how it's impossible to eat well and economically in Venice have circulated for decades, misinforming day trippers clinging defensively to their pizza slices in San Marco. Little do they realise that for the same price they could be dining on crostini topped with scampi and grilled baby artichoke, or tuna tartare with wild strawberries and a balsamic reduction.

Once you know what to look for, Venice becomes a foodie treasure hunt. Beware any menu dotted with asterisks indicating that items are *surgelati* (frozen). Lasagne, spaghetti Bolognese and pizza are not Venetian specialities, so avoid any tourist trap where all three appear on the menu. Look for places where there's no menu at all, or one hastily scrawled on a chalkboard or laser-printed in Italian only. This is a sign your chef reinvents the menu daily according to what's on offer at the market.

Your favourite meals may be eaten standing up at 6.30pm, the moment *cicheti* are put out at many *bacari*. However, you should treat yourself to one leisurely sit-down meal while you're in Venice, whether it's in a back-alley *osteria* or a canalside restaurant. You'll win over your waiter and the chef by doing the following:

Ignore the menu. Solicit your server's advice about seasonal treats and house specials, pick two options that sound interesting, and ask your server to recommend one over the other. When that's done, snap the menu shut and say, '*Allora, facciamo cosi, per favore!*' (Well then, let's do that, please!) You have just made your waiter's day and flattered the chef.

Drink well. Bottled water is optional (local *acqua al rubinetto,* tap water, is perfectly drinkable) but fine meals call for wine, which is often available by the glass or half bottle. Don't worry if you don't recognise the label; the best small-production local wineries don't advertise or export, because their entire yield is snapped up by Venetian *osterie.*

Try primi *(first courses) without condiments.* Your waiter's relief and delight will be obvious – Venetian seafood pastas are rich and flavourful enough without being smothered in Parmesan or hot sauce.

Go with local seafood. No one expects you to order an appetiser or *secondo piatto* (second course), but if you do, the tests of any Venetian chef are fish antipasti and *frittura* (fried seafood). Try yours *senza limone* (without lemon) first; Venetians believe the delicate flavours of their seafood are best complemented by salt and pepper.

BEST CICHETI

> All'Arco (p91)
> I Rusteghi (p55)
> Alla Vedova (p77)
> Pronto Pesce Pronto (p94)
> Dai Zemei (p92)

BEST INVENTIVE VENETIAN

> Al Fontego dei Pescatori (p75)
> I Figli delle Stelle (p130)
> Trattoria Corte Sconta (p68)
> Sangal (p54)
> Il Ridotto (p67)

BEST TRADITIONAL VENETIAN

> Al Covo (p66)
> Ristoteca Oniga (p121)
> Trattoria al Gatto Nero (p147)
> Vini da Gigio (p79)
> Vecio Fritolin (p106)

BEST SPECIALITY JOINTS

> Alaska Gelateria (p104) for gelato
> **Ristorante** La Bitta (p120) for meat
> Osteria La Zucca (p105) for veggie dishes
> Zenzero (p68) for pastries
> Snack Bar ai Nomboli (p95) for panini

ARCHITECTURE

Lulls in conversation in Venice are easily resolved with one innocent question: what is Venetian architecture? Venice's cosmopolitan flair defines its architecture, from the 7th- and 9th-century Byzantine Cattedrale di Santa Maria Assunta (p144) on Torcello to Tadao Ando's 2008 reinvention of the Punta della Dogana customs houses (p114). An East–West landmark that defies any single genre, the Basilica di San Marco (p41) covers every style from Byzantine Constantinople to 19th-century Renaissance revival. In contrast, Venice's Gothic I Frari (p84), Zanipolo (p64) and Chiesa della Madonna dell'Orto (p74) are actually more austere than their French cousins. The Venetian Renaissance revived classical ideas under Jacopo Sansovino (1486–1570) and Andrea Palladio (1508–80), who combined classical geometry with a generous baroque sense of interior space in Chiesa di San Giorgio Maggiore (p126) and Il Redentore (p128). But just when Venetian architecture began to seem set in its classicising ways, Baldassare Longhena (1598–1682) redefined 17th-century baroque with his Roman-and-cabbala-inspired Chiesa di Santa Maria della Salute (p109).

Everyone has a pet period in Venice's chequered architectural history. Ruskin waxed rhapsodic about Byzantine Gothic Basilica di San Marco, and detested Palladio and his Chiesa di San Giorgio Maggiore; Palladians rebuffed rococo; fans of the regal rococo of Ca' Rezzonico were scandalised by the Lido's bohemian Liberty style; and pretty much everyone was horrified by the inclinations of industry to strip Venice of its ornamentation.

After Giudecca's baroque buildings were torn down for factories, the city took decades to recover from the shock. Architects reverted to venezianitá, a tendency to tack on to buildings exaggerated Venetian elements from a range of periods – a Gothic trefoil arch here, a baroque cupola there. Rather than using the interiors of the buildings to harmonise these disparate architectural elements, Venetians swagged them in silk damask and lit them with Murano chandeliers. The resulting hotchpotch seemed to signal the end of Venice's architectural glory days.

Then came the flood of 1966, and it seemed all of Venice's architectural patrimony would be lost. Architecture aficionados around the globe put aside their differences, and aided Venetians to bail out *palazzi* and reinforce foundations across the city. With preservation efforts and postmodernism came a fresh approach to Venice's composite architecture; rather than tearing down one style or wallpapering over differences, architects chose spare modern treatments to creatively repurpose the past. With this approach, the Fondazione Giorgio Cini converted a naval academy into a gallery, while Tadao Ando has turned the Punta della Dogana customs houses into a contemporary-art showplace.

BEST ARCHITECTURAL LANDMARKS
> Basilica di San Marco (p41)
> Chiesa di San Giorgio Maggiore (p126)
> Ducal Palace (p45)
> Chiesa di Santa Maria dei Miracoli (p74)
> Chiesa di Santa Maria della Salute (p109)

BEST MODERN ARCHITECTURE
> Palazzo Grassi (p47)
> Biennale pavilions (p59)
> Fondazione Querini Stampalia (p59)
> Fondazione Giorgio Cini (p127)
> Punta della Dogana (p114)

Top left Gorgeously Gothic Ducal Palace (p45) **Above** A healthy sense of proportion at Chiesa di Santa Maria della Salute (p109)

ARTISANS

It may be hard to describe your Venice souvenirs without sounding like you're bragging. 'It's an original,' you'll say, 'and I met the artisan.' While artisanal traditions across the rest of the industrialised world have disappeared or been fossilised into relics of bygone eras, Venetians have kept their craft tradition alive, innovative and surprisingly accessible.

From clever *carta marmorizzata* (marbled-paper) travel journals (€12) to custom-made red-carpet shoes (€200), Venice's handcrafted goods are reasonably priced for the labour involved; costs are competitive with mass-produced merchandise that has logos in lieu of individual personality. Paris' latest It bags seem uninspired compared to Venetian purses made from marbled paper or silk-screened velvet, and Tiffany jewellery seems ho-hum once you've glimpsed the glass-ring selection in Murano.

So how did you come by that Venetian heirloom piece, you crafty shopper? First you had to know where to look: down the back alleys of San Polo, Santa Croce, Dorsoduro, San Marco, Castello and Murano, and inside the studios and showrooms of local artisans. Studios tend to cluster together, so getting lost in an artisans' area is a great way to find unique pieces. Showrooms filled with glass and shelves of fragile handicrafts may be labelled *Non Toccare* (Don't Touch) – instead of risking breakage, just ask the staff to show you the pieces. The person who shows it to you may be the very person who made it, so don't be shy about saying *'Complimenti!'* (My compliments!) for impressive pieces. In a world of knock offs and cookie-cutter culture, your support for these handicrafts is a vote for Venice's enduring originality.

BEST VENICE ORIGINALS

> Book-bound handbags at Carté (p87)
> Enamelled skull earrings at Sigfrido Cipolato (p66)
> Leather plague-doctor masks at La Pietra Filosofale (p50)
> Gondola prows at Ervas (p103)
> Bohemian-chic textiles at Fortuny Tessuti Artistici (p128)

BEST GLASS DESIGNS

> Glass-studded necklaces at Marina e Susanna Sent (p118)
> Glass mosquitoes at I Vetri a Lume di Amadi (p89)
> Liquid-crystal vases at ElleElle (p145)
> Satin-finish glass teardrop necklaces at Esperienze (p49)
> Circus-striped glass beads at Campagnol & Salvadore (p145)

MUSIC & OPERA

Over the centuries, Venetian musicians developed a reputation for playing music as though their lives depended on it. In its heyday, Venice had official musicians and distinct party music, but it was only when it fell on hard times in the 17th and 18th centuries that it really discovered its musical talents. With shrinking trade revenues, the state underwrote the musical education of orphan girls, and the investment yielded extraordinary returns. Visitors spread word of superb performances by the girls, and Venice's reputation for music made it a magnet for socialites.

Today's televised talent searches can't compare to Venice's ability to discover musical talents, including Claudio Monteverdi, who was named the musical director of the Basilica di San Marco and went on to launch modern opera. Similarly, one of the maestri hired to conduct the orphan-girl orchestras was Antonio Vivaldi, who in the course of his 30-year tenure wrote hundreds of concertos and popularised Venetian music across Europe.

Modern visitors to Venice can still see music performed in much the same venues as it was in Vivaldi's day – *palazzi,* churches and *ospedaletti* (orphanages). But rather than playing classical music or opera as period pieces, Venice's leading interpreters perform with verve and wit, keeping up their end of a musical conversation that began centuries ago.

BEST PERFORMANCES & VENUES

> Teatro La Fenice (p57)
> Musica a Palazzo (p57) in Palazzo Barbarigo-Minotto
> Interpreti Veneziani (p56) at San Vidal
> Collegium Ducale (p69) in Prigioni Nuove
> Venice International Festival of Contemporary Music (p30) inside Arsenale shipbuilding warehouses

BEST MUSICAL MEMENTOS

> Singing lessons through the Venetian Club (p121)
> Harmonicas and lutes from Mille e Una Nota (p89)
> Clothes based on costumes worn by La Fenice divas from Banco 10 (p65)
> CDs from Parole e Musica (p65)
> Vivaldi biographies from Libreria Studium (p50)

SHOPPING

Churches and museums are all well and good, but who are we kidding? In Italy anyone with the faintest retail inclination is going to wind up in a store eventually. That doesn't mean you have to end up with one of those glittered porcelain-mask magnets or a striped gondolier shirt (though, hey, those can be quite hip out of context). In Venice you can find gifts by local artisans that truly are one of a kind; the odds of a work-mate showing up to the Christmas party in the same locally designed Fortuny frock or Fiorella smoking jacket are infinitesimal.

Mall shopping just can't compare to treasure hunting in Venice. Sure, there are the standard Italian designer brands along Via Larga XXII Marzo and Calle dei Fabbri in San Marco, but the rarest finds and sweetest deals await across the Grand Canal in the backstreet boutiques of San Polo and Dorsoduro. Open-air markets reveal hidden gems – exquisite enamelled lockets or an actual pirate's pipe – and at fair-trade boutiques your sun-hat purchase supports a worthy cause. Depending on your country's customs regulations, Venetian edibles and wines make tasteful souvenirs.

BEST FOR FASHION
> Fiorella Gallery (p49)
> Venetia Studium (p51)
> Arnoldo & Battois (p48)
> Ottica Carraro (p51)
> Giovanna Zanella (p65)

BEST FEEL-GOOD RETAIL
> Banco 10 (p65)
> Venice's artisans (p158)
> Le Botteghe (p49)
> Aqua Altra (p115)
> Mercato delle pulci (p114)

BEST ART & ANTIQUES
> Caterina Tognon Arte Contemporanea (p44)
> Jarach Gallery (p46)
> Galleria Traghetto (p45)
> Campiello Ca' Zen (p87)
> Mercantino dei Miracoli (p114)

BEST HOMEWARES
> Madera (p117)
> Neropaco (p145)
> Danghyra (p117)
> Bochaleri in Giardini (p114)
> Epicentro (p49)

RELIGIOUS EXPERIENCES

After a few blissful days of wandering this fair city, the same thought occurs to most visitors: thank heaven for Venice. This is no coincidence. Soaring Venetian Gothic arches and rooftop synagogue cupolas direct the eye heavenward, museums are packed with masterpieces based on religious themes, and angels are in the architecture at street-corner shrines and *scuole* (religious confraternities). Venetians grateful for surviving plagues, floods and invasions showed their appreciation in monumental form, building 107 churches and seven synagogues where they could give thanks on a regular basis.

As if that weren't enough, pontoon bridges are strung across canals for festivals such as Festa del Redentore (p29) and Festa della Madonna della Salute (p30), when Venetians risk a dunking to light candles for the survival of their city. On saints' days – and at every opportunity – Venetians celebrate with sweet treats and toasts to the *bea vita* (good life).

With all this divine inspiration, where do you begin? Basilica di San Marco (p41) is an obvious choice, but the Museo delle Icone (p59) and the Museo Ebraico di Venezia (p74) show the diversity of Venice's religious traditions. Island retreats such as the San Giorgio Maggiore cloisters (p126) show true devotion, but so do smaller neighbourhood institutions such as Chiesa di Santa Maria dei Miracoli (p74) and Chiesa di San Sebastian (p109).

BEST DIVINE INSPIRATIONS

> Mosaics at Basilica di San Marco (p41)
> *Madonna of the Assumption* at I Frari (p84)
> *The Last Judgment* at Chiesa della Madonna dell'Orto (p74)
> Longhena's stairway to heaven at Scuola Grande dei Carmini (p114)
> The women's gallery of the Spanish Schola synagogue (synagogue tour, p75)

BEST HEAVENLY INDULGENCES

> Balsamic-vinegar chocolate truffles at VizioVirtù (p91)
> *Zaete* (biscuits) and *krapfen* (doughnuts) at Festa della Madonna della Salute (p30)
> Mid-Biennale macchiato at Paradiso (p69)
> Amalfi lemon sorbet at Grom (p119)
> Prosecco and poetry at Sacro e Profano (p94)

OFF-SEASON VENICE

Winter is the most stirring movement of Vivaldi's *Four Seasons* for a reason – the composer had great source material. Just think of footsteps muffled by snow, icicles dripping from Venetian Gothic windows, and boots being stamped at the doorsteps of buzzing *bacari*. This is the season when Venetians let down their guard, bored chefs sit and chat over lunch, and artisans in their studios are glad of any interruption. Intrepid travellers may have Piazza San Marco to themselves as they skid across patches of ice in their rush to get to gooey hot chocolate.

There are also practical advantages to visiting Venice between November and March. Except at Christmas and Carnevale, prices are slashed on everything from accommodation and excursions to dinners and drinks. Museums have fewer visitors, and restaurants offer limited menus to mostly local crowds – which has a definite upside. Finally you can skip the queues and take in Titians at the Accademia and futurists at the Peggy Guggenheim Collection without meekly following the tour-group herds, then strike up conversations about Venetian colour over drinks afterwards.

BEST OFF-SEASON THINGS TO DO
> Learn Italian at Istituto Venezia (p121)
> Attend Biennale closing parties (p17)
> Cross the Grand Canal at Festa della Madonna della Salute (p30)
> Warm up by a blazing fire watching glassblowers at Murano furnaces (p141)
> Celebrate Carnevale in costume at Teatro La Fenice (p57)

BEST SEASONAL SPECIALITIES
> *Anatra* (lagoon duck)
> *Moscardini* (baby octopus)
> *Granseola* (spider crab)
> *Radicchio di Treviso*
> *Fritole* (sweet fritters)

BEST OFF-SEASON TRAVEL ADVANTAGES
> Leisurely conversations with Venetians
> Last-minute tickets to La Fenice (p57)
> Reservations at the restaurant of your choice
> No lines at the Accademia (p112)
> Winter light inside San Marco (p41)

BEST WAYS TO STAY WARM
> Hot chocolate at VizioVirtù (p91)
> *Brodo di pesce* (saffron-scented fish stew) at Anice Stellato (p77)
> *Pasta e fasioi* (pasta with beans) at La Cantina (p78)
> *Caffè corretto* (coffee 'corrected' with brandy) at Caffè Florian (p56)
> Vintage Amarone at I Rusteghi (p55)

HANDS-ON VENICE

After you ogle your third Titian and 10th gondola, you may start to get ideas of your own. Technically you can't touch a Titian, and it takes years to become a gondolier, but the traditions of painting and boating are perfectly within reach. Even if gondolas and frescoes won't fit into your luggage, a model boat by Gilberto Penzo and paints from Arcobaleno might. Other souvenirs will pass even the toughest carry-on restrictions: an eye for colour developed at a printmaking workshop, an ear for baroque music discovered at a musical course, or a sense of balance lost and found the hard way through *voga alla veneta* (rowing standing up, Venetian style).

Inspiration is sprinkled across Venice, and it would be a shame to let it go to waste. Designing your own wine tasting is easy at local *enoteche* (wine bars), while a cooking class will allow you to take *cicheti* home (see www.veneceto gourmet.com). Glass-blowing takes commitment, but you can create lampworked beads and glass mosaics in short courses through the Venetian Club (p121). If this city on the water has one standing lesson to offer, it's that imagination makes anything possible.

BEST THINGS TO TRY
> Capture Venice in moody aquatints at Bottega del Tintoretto (p81)
> Row standing up on the lagoon with Row Venice's Jane Caporal (p143)
> Compare Veneto vintages with a wine tasting at L'Orto dei Mori (p78)
> Bind your own marble-paper photo album with Ebrù (p48)
> Learn mask-making secrets at Ca' Macana (p121)

BEST FOR DIY SUPPLIES
> Arcobaleno (p48) for art
> Mare di Carta (p103) for sailing
> Gilberto Penzo (p88) for toy boats
> Drogheria Mascari (p87) for cooking
> Rialto produce markets (p94) for picnics and still-life paintings

SNAPSHOTS

CIN-CIN

No rules seem to apply to drinking in Venice. Happy hour from 6pm to 7pm? More like twice daily, from 11am to 3pm and 6.30pm to 8.30pm. No mixing spirits and wine? Venice's classic cocktails, such as *spritz* (made with prosecco, plus Aperol or Campari), suggest otherwise. No girly drinks? Tell that to burly boat builders enjoying a frothy prosecco.

This makes knowing what to order where a little tricky. Price is not an indicator of quality – you can pay €2 for a respectable *spritz,* or live to regret that €15 Bellini (ouch). If you're not pleased with your drink, leave it and move on to the next *bacaro*. Venice is too small and life too short to make do with ho-hum hooch.

In the rest of Italy, the DOC *(denominazione d'origine controllata)* and elite DOCG *(denominazione d'origine controllata e garantita)* designations are usually assurances of top-notch *vino*, but Veneto bucks the system. Several small-production Veneto wineries can't be bothered with such external validation, because they already sell out to Venetian *osterie* and *enoteche*. Even ordinary varietals take on extraordinary characteristics in the unusual Veneto growing regions, so a merlot or soave could be the most adventurous choice on the menu.

Happily, *osterie* and *enoteche* sell good stuff by the glass or half bottle, so you can discover new favourites without committing to a whole bottle. Even budding oenologists should solicit suggestions from *osterie* hosts, who'll accept the challenge of finding your new favourite Venetian tipple as a point of local pride. *Cin-cin* – bottoms up.

BEST VENETO WINES TO TRY

> Prosecco – the sparkling white that's the life of any Venetian party
> Valpolicella Classico – the chef's choice: a versatile, virtuoso red
> Lugana – a well-structured, minerally white worthy of Palladio
> Raboso del Piave – brash when young, brilliant with age
> Amarone – a profound, voluptuous red

BEST SIGNATURE DRINKS

> Spritz at Caffè Rosso (p122)
> Rialto at B Bar (p54)
> Danieli at Bar Terazza Danieli (p68)
> Bellini at Harry's Dolci (p130)
> Water bottles filled with wine from the barrel at Nave d'Oro (p95)

>BACKGROUND

The Museo Storico Navale (p62) holds golden memories of Venice's glorious history

BACKGROUND

BACKGROUND

HISTORY

FROM SWAMP TO EMPIRE

A malarial swamp is a strange place to put a city – unless you're under attack by Huns and Goths. And so began the story of Venice in AD 452. Crafty settlers soon rose above their swampy circumstances, residing on land that was lifted above tides by wooden pylons driven into some 30m of soft silt.

Once terra firma was established, Venice set about shoring up its business interests. While rival Genoa was busy charting routes to the New World, Venice concentrated on controlling the last leg of the spice and silk trade routes to Europe. Jealous Genoa tried to take over the city and its maritime trade in 1380, after Venice was weakened by the plague. But Venice prevailed, and the city soon controlled a backyard that stretched from Dalmatia to Bergamo.

By the mid-15th century, Venice was swathed in golden mosaics and rustling silks, and doused in incense to cover the belching sulphuric smells that were the downside of a lagoon empire. La Serenissima (the Most Serene) retained its calm during this time with a complex system of checks and balances, plus bouts of outright repression: the Great Council elected a doge to preside over council matters, while Venice's shadowy secret service, the Consiglio dei Dieci (Council of Ten), thwarted conspiracies with a network of spies.

TRENDSETTERS & TROUBLEMAKERS

As Venice lost ground to pirates and Ottomans, the city again rose to the occasion, conquering Europe by charm instead. Venice's art was

BETTER THAN BOND

Venice made a killing in the Crusades as a triple agent, accepting a Frankish commission of 84,000 silver marks to wrest the Holy Land from Muslim control, but continuing to trade with Muslim powers from Syria to Spain. But when the balance of the Frankish commission wasn't forthcoming, Venice decided to claim Constantinople with the aid of the Franks. While the city was ostensibly claimed for Christendom, Venice also benefited: ships loaded with booty were sent back home.

ROXANNE, YOU *DO* HAVE TO PUT OUT THE RED LIGHT

Venetian courtesans were widely admired taste makers and poets in the 14th century, so the city's idea of a crackdown was to decree that ladies of the night should have red lights attached to their gondolas, and should only display their wares in windows from the waist up rather than baring all in the streets. By the end of the 16th century, the town was flush with some 12,000 registered prostitutes, creating a literal red-light district. Today, however, red beacons mostly signal construction – but you can enjoy a decadent dinner at Antiche Carampane (the Old Streetwalkers; p92), near Ponte delle Tette (Tits Bridge).

incredibly daring, bringing sensuous colour and sly social commentary to familiar religious subjects, while Venetian music (p159) was irresistibly catchy, instigating a merry mingling of men and women, Italians and Germans, clergy and socialites.

Church authorities were not amused, and repeatedly censured Venetians for depicting holy subjects in an earthy Venetian light and for playing toe-tapping tunes in churches. But, in 1767, after persistent reproaches from Rome, Venice calculated the amount of revenue that it had rendered to Rome in the previous decade; the result was a grand total of 11 million golden ducats. Venice promptly closed 127 monasteries and convents, cutting the local clerical population by 50% and redirecting to the city's coffers millions of ducats that would otherwise have gone to Rome.

Meanwhile, Venetian tastes and trends stealthily took over drawing rooms across the continent, and the city became a playground for Europe's upper crust. Nunneries in Venice held soirées to rival those in its *ridotti* (casinos), and Carnevale lasted up to three months. Venetian 'white widows' with husbands at sea took young, handsome *cicisbei* (young manservants) to tend their needs. Not coincidentally, Venetian ladies also occasionally fell into religious fervours entailing a nine-month seclusion, and abandoned orphans soon filled four well-funded *ospedaletti* (orphanages). By the 18th century, less than 40% of Venetian nobles bothered with the formality of marriage, and the regularity of Venetian annulments scandalised even visiting French courtiers.

PARTY'S OVER

By the time Napoleon arrived in 1797, Venice had been reduced by plague and circumstance from 175,000 people to fewer than 100,000, and the Venetians' reputation as fierce partiers did nothing to prevent the French and Austrians from handing the city back and forth as a trophy. By 1817, one-quarter of Venice's population was destitute, and when Venice rallied to resist the Austrians in 1848–49, the Austrians' blockade left it wracked by cholera and short on food. The indignity of it all would fester until Venice joined the Kingdom of Italy in 1866.

The glamorous city took on a workaday aspect in the 19th and 20th centuries. Factories were added on Giudecca, a railway bridge was built, and Mussolini added a roadway from the mainland, literally bringing Venice into line with the rest of Italy. Venice capitulated to Fascism and Allied troops in turn, and the war and the shock of the mass deportation of the city's Jewish population in 1943–44 helped precipitate an urban identity crisis. By 1966, Venetians were abandoning the city for Milan and other postwar economic centres, and Venice seemed as forlorn as a party where invited guests had decided they had better things to do.

ALTA ACQUA

Then, on 4 November 1966, disaster struck. Record floods poured into 16,000 Venetian homes in terrifying waves, and residents were stranded in the wreckage of 1400 years of civilisation. But Venice refused to be mired in despair, instead calling on its many admirers for aid. Assistance poured in from Mexico to Australia, and from millionaires and pensioners alike; Unesco coordinated some 27 private organisations to redress the ravages of the flood. Photographs of the era (available online at www .albumdivenezia.it) show Venetians drying ancient books one page at a time, and gondolas gliding into bars for *spritz* (prosecco-based cocktails) served by bartenders in hip-high waders.

TOP FIVE FILMS SET IN VENICE

> *Pane e Tulipani (Bread and Tulips)* – An AWOL housewife starts life anew in Venice.
> *Casanova* – The story of the philanderer's life; watch the Fellini version with Donald Sutherland rather than Lasse Hallstrom's take (despite Heath Ledger's winsome presence).
> *Don't Look Now* – Julie Christie and Donald Sutherland's demons follow them to Venice in Nicolas Roeg's taut thriller.
> *Casino Royale* – The action-packed finale in this film takes James Bond down the Grand Canal (don't worry, that palace survived).
> *Death in Venice* – Luchino Visconti takes on Thomas Mann's story of a Mahler-esque composer, an infatuation and a deadly outbreak of disease.

NOALTRÍ V VOALTRÍ (US VERSUS THEM)

The usual outsider–insider dynamic doesn't quite wash in cosmopolitan Venice, whose excellent taste in imports ranges from Byzantine mosaics to the Venice Film Festival. Bringing a world-class art collection with you is one way to fit in, as Peggy Guggenheim and François Pinault discovered. But you don't have to be a mogul to *venexianárse* (become Venetian). Of the 20 million visitors to Venice each year, only some three million stay overnight; staying in a locally run B&B (p150) is a chance to experience Venice among Venetians. In addition, you can eat like a Venetian (p154), attempt a few words of Venetian dialect (p178) or learn a Venetian craft (p163). But the surest way to win over Venetians is to express curiosity about them and their city – so few day trippers stop to make polite conversation that any attempt is received with surprise and appreciation. As you'll soon find out, those other 17 million visitors are missing out on excellent company.

Venice's *alta acqua* (high-water) bravado may be its saving grace at a time when the population has continued to leave the city for the lower rents and job opportunities on the mainland, and cruise ships inundate the city with day trippers. But despite dire predictions, Venice has not yet become a Disneyland version of itself or a lost Atlantis. The city remains relevant and realistic, continuing to produce new music, art and crafts even as it seeks sustainable solutions to its rising water levels (p172). Venice today is anchored not merely by its ancient pylons, but by the people who put them there: the Venetians.

LIFE AS A VENETIAN

Look around: all those splendid palaces, paintings and churches were created by a handful of Venetians. In the city's entire history, there have only been about three million Venetians who could claim grandparents from Venice. With the 60,000 official residents easily outnumbered by visitors on any given day, Venetians may seem like a rarity in their own city. The population has halved in size since 1848, and 25% of the population is over 65. But there are 2000 children still playing tag in Venice's *campi* (squares), and local universities keep the city young and full of ideas. If you don't always encounter locals on the main thoroughfares it's because Venetians prefer to *andare per le fodere* (to go by the inner linings) of the city's 3000 backstreets.

Despite its reputation, this is not just a city of the idle rich. Most Venetians live in flats, and 1000 Venetian palaces are now used as hotels and

BACKGROUND

B&Bs. Hard-working Venetians pursue artisanal occupations that might sound esoteric: paper marbling, glass-blowing, octopus fishing. But they are constantly reinventing these traditions, and in tiny storefronts you can glimpse artisans turning paper into a purse, glass into jewellery, and baby octopi into brilliant *cicheti* (Venetian tapas). Resting on past glories would be easy, while topping them seems impossible – but, as usual, Venetians are opting for the impossible.

ART

The sheer number of masterpieces packed into Venice might make you wonder if there's something in the water here. The reason may be more simple: historically, Venice tended not to starve its artists. Rather than suffering for their art, many Venetian artists and architects did quite well by it. So instead of dying young and destitute, painters such as Titian and Giovanni Bellini, and architects such as Jacopo Sansovino and Baldassare Longhena, all survived into their eighties to produce late, great works. (For more on architecture, see p156.)

Venice's guild of house painters included some of art history's greatest names. One dues-paying member, Giovanni Bellini (c 1430–1516), passed on his tremendous skills with human expression and glowing colour to two rather apt pupils: Giorgione (1477–1510) and Titian (c 1490–1576), whose work can be compared in the Accademia (p112). Vittore Carpaccio (1460–1526) rivalled Titian's reds with his own sanguine hues, but it was Titian's Madonna of the Ascension in I Frari (p84) that cemented Venice's reputation for glorious colour.

TOP FIVE BOOKS SET IN VENICE

> *Shakespeare in Venice* by Alberto Toso Fei – A captivating guide to the Venetian inspirations for Shakespeare's dramas, including *Othello* and *Merchant of Venice*.
> *The Passion* by Jeanette Winterson – Napoleon's cook pursues a card-dealing Venetian woman of mystery in this magic-realist fable.
> *Invisible Cities* by Italo Calvino – Venetian explorer Marco Polo tells Kublai Khan of his travels across the globe – yet every city he describes is Venice.
> *Corto Maltese: Fable of Venice* by Hugo Pratt – The Italian comic-book legend's cosmopolitan sea captain cracks the mysteries of the *calli* (streets).
> *The Story of My Life* by Giacomo Casanova – The notorious Venetian seducer, gambler, amateur necromancer and escaped political prisoner tells all.

But though art history tends to insist on a division of labour between Venice and Florence – Venice had the colour, Florence the ideas – the Venetian school had plenty of ideas that repeatedly got it into trouble. Tintoretto may have earned key public commissions, but his lightning-bolt brushwork, which drew out human drama even in religious scenes, proved controversial. The luminous colours of Paolo Veronese (1528–88) were never in question, but his decision to depict Germans, Turks, gamblers and dogs among the saints in *The Last Supper* drew censure from the Church. He refused to change the picture, instead renaming it *Feast in the House of Levi*.

Pietro Longhi (1701–85) dispensed with the premise of lofty subject matter and painted Venetian social satires, while Giambattista Tiepolo (1696–1770) turned religious themes into a premise for dizzying ceilings covered with rococo sunbursts. Many Venetian artists turned their attention from the heavens to the local landscape, notably Canaletto (1697–1768). And, instead of drawing popes on thrones, portraitist Rosalba Carriera (1675–1757) captured her socialite sitters on snuffboxes.

ENVIRONMENT

With 400 bridges connecting 117 islets across 200 canals, Venice's natural setting is extraordinary – and extraordinarily fragile. The whole set-up is protected only by a slender arc of islands that halts the Adriatic's advances.

You may have heard that Venice is sinking, but that's not entirely accurate. The city is partially built on wooden foundations sunk deep into lagoon silt, and it's held up miraculously well for centuries. But the foundations are taking a pounding as never before, with new stresses coming from industrial pollutants and wakes of speeding motorboats. At the same time, the dredging of deeper channels to accommodate supertankers and cruise ships has contributed to the rise in water levels doubling since 1900. Back then, Piazza San Marco flooded about 10 times a year; now it's closer to 60. Technology advances have helped keep Venice afloat, and engineers now estimate that Venice may be able to withstand a 26cm to 60cm rise in water levels in the 21st century – which is great news, except for the fact that an intergovernmental panel on climate change recently forecasted increases as great as 88cm.

Complex solutions aren't easy, but simple gestures are. Recycling your waste and tidying as you go through Venice will be appreciated; when

TO MOSE, OR NOT TO MOSE?

The hot topic of the last 30 years in Venice has been a mobile-flood-barrier project known as MOSE. Ever since the great flood of 1966, many Unesco-affiliated agencies have been urgently concerned about this jewel box of a city, which contains many of the world's great art treasures, and MOSE proponents say the city must be saved at any cost.

With estimated costs topping €5.5 billion, the 30m-high and 20m-wide inflatable barriers are intended to seal the three entrances to Venice's lagoon whenever the sea approaches dangerous levels. This is only a partial solution, however, since flooding is also caused by excessive rain and swollen inland rivers.

But, as many Venetians are quick to point out, the city is their home, not just a treasure chest, and the impact of any stop-gap measure must be considered. Would flood barriers fill the lagoon with stagnant water, creating public-health risks and driving away tourists? Could MOSE change local aquaculture, ending fishing on the Unesco-protected lagoon? Will it delay solutions to underlying problems?

Originally planned for 2010, MOSE completion is scheduled for 2014. Meanwhile, local environmentalists are keenly tracking the impact of global warming, cruise ships and pollution from the Marghera petrochemical plant on water levels, fishing prospects and everyday life in Venice.

receptacles are scarce or full, take your rubbish with you. Spare the city the effort of recycling some 20 to 60 million water bottles annually by insisting on tap water. Gondoliers will sing your praises if you ask water-taxi drivers to go slower to avoid kicking up a wake. Spend time and money in locally owned businesses, and you'll be assuring your Venetian hosts that all their effort to maintain the city is worthwhile.

DIRECTORY
TRANSPORT
ARRIVAL & DEPARTURE
AIR

Most flights arrive on the mainland at **Marco Polo Airport** (VCF; ☎ 041 2609260; www.veniceairport.it), 12km from Venice. Low-cost airlines are a benefit to travellers, but a burden on the environment and Venice's air quality; to travel with a cleaner conscience, consider a carbon-offset program (see below).

See p174 for information on getting to/from the airport.

TRAIN

Prompt, affordable, scenic and environmentally friendly, trains are an excellent way to travel to and from Venice. Trains run frequently to Venice's Stazione Santa Lucia (signed as Ferrovia within Venice) from major European cities and locations throughout Italy, and most vaporetti (city ferries) stop right outside the station. Tickets for all trains can be purchased at self-serve ticketing machines in the station, online at www.trenitalia .it, or at **Rail Europe** (☎ 0844 8484064; www.raileurope.co.uk) in the UK.

GETTING AROUND

Major destinations within Venice are rarely more than a 10- to 30-minute walk away, not including photo and gelato pit stops. **Azienda Consorzio Trasporti Veneziano** (ACTV; www.actv.it) organises the vaporetto network that runs inside Venice and to outlying islands, including Giudecca, Lido, Murano, Burano and Torcello. In this book, the nearest vaporetto stop is noted after the 🚢 in each listing.

TRAVEL PASSES

If you're planning to use public transport often, buy a

CLIMATE CHANGE & TRAVEL

Travel – especially air travel – is a significant contributor to global climate change. At Lonely Planet, we believe that all who travel have a responsibility to limit their personal impact. As a result, we have teamed with Rough Guides and other concerned industry partners to support Climate Care, which allows people to offset the greenhouse gases they are responsible for with contributions to energy-saving projects and other climate-friendly initiatives in the developing world. Lonely Planet offsets all staff and author travel.

For more information, turn to the responsible travel pages on www.lonelyplanet .com. For details on offsetting your carbon emissions and a carbon calculator, go to www .climatecare.org.

DIRECTORY

TRAVEL TO/FROM THE AIRPORT

	Ferry	ATVO Fly Bus	ACTV bus 5	Water taxi
Pick-up point	at the dock, located a 10min walk from terminal	in front of terminal	in front of terminal	at the dock, located a 10min walk from terminal
Drop-off point	direct to San Marco (Oro line) or Blu, Rossa and Arancio lines with multiple stops (eg Fondamente Nuove, San Zaccaria, Zattere, Giudecca; see website for routes	Piazzale Roma	Piazzale Roma	nearest dock to hotel
Duration	50-80min, depending on destination	20min	40min	30-50min, depending on destination
Cost	€13 one-way standard or €30 Oro service	€3	€1	depends on destination and number of passengers; usually €90-120 for 4 people
Other	purchase tickets in terminal or at dock, or get discounted tickets online at www .venicelink.com	departs every 30-50min; purchase tickets at Piazzale Roma or the terminal	makes frequent mainland stops; purchase tickets at Piazzale Roma or the terminal	for advance bookings, try Airport Link shared water taxi service (€30 one-way) at www .venicelink.com, or ask at your hotel reception about sharing an airport taxi with other hotel guests
Contact	www.alilaguna.com	www.atvo.it	www.actv.it	☎ 041 5222303, 041 5221265

biglietto a tempo (12/24/36/48/72hr ticket €16/18/23/28/33, 7-day ticket €50), a timed ticket that allows unlimited access to most vaporetti (except longer-distance Alilaguna, Clodia, Fusina and LineaBlù lines) plus Lido and Mestre buses for the stated timeframe, starting after you validate your ticket in dockside validation machines. Tickets can be purchased at **Hellovenezia** (☎ 041 2424; www.hellovenezia.com; ✆ call centre 8am-7.30pm) ticket booths at **Stazione Santa Lucia** (Map pp72-3, B5; Cannaregio; ✆ 7am-8.30pm), **Piazzale Roma** (Map pp100-1, B3; Santa Croce), and vaporetto stops at Ferrovia, Rialto, Accademia, San Marco and San Zaccaria.

Hellovenezia also offers **VENICEcard transport & culture passes** (junior/senior 3-day €66/73, 7-day €87/96) that entitles holders to unlimited use of vaporetti during the stated period, plus free entry to 12 civic museums and 16 churches, public pay toilet access, plus discounts on select cultural events. VENICE-card can be purchased at **Azienda di Promozione Turistica** (APT; Map pp42-3, G5; ☎ 041 5298711; www.turismovenezia .it; Piazza San Marco 71f, San Marco; ⏰ 9am-3.30pm Mon-Sat; 🚤 San Marco) or Hellovenezia ticket outlets.

For travellers aged 15 to 29, **Rolling VeniceCard** (pass €4) allows you to buy a 72-hour public-transport pass for €18 and provides discounted access to monuments and cultural events. The pass can be purchased at Hellovenezia ticket booths; identification is required.

VAPORETTO
Several vaporetto lines run up and down the Grand Canal, some with faster *limitato* (limited-stop) service. Line 1 makes all stops between Ferrovia and San Marco in about 30 to 45 minutes. Tickets should be bought in advance and validated prior to boarding in the yellow machines located dockside. Single-trip tickets cost €6.50, so

travel passes (above) offer good value. Timetables are available online at www.actv.it/english/ home.php and are posted at stops; next departures are often listed at the stops on digital displays. Some lines start as early as 5.30am, while others stop as early as 9pm. A night (N) service runs along the Grand Canal and serves the Lido and Giudecca, but all services stop at 4.30am.

TRAGHETTO
Get your gondola ride on the cheap. Both picturesque and prac-tical, *traghetti* are large commuter gondolas that cross the Grand Canal at set spots for €2 per passenger. But there are no seats – everyone crosses standing. Some operate from about 9am to 6pm, while others stop at around noon. Look for *traghetto* signs on *calli* (streets) parallel to the Grand Canal.

GONDOLA
More than a way to get from point A to point B, a gondola trip is an insight into a hidden Venice that is anything but pedestrian, offering rare peeks into *palazzi* (palaces or mansions) and courtyards. Official rates for 40 minutes are €80 during the day or €100 from 7pm to 8am, not including opera arias (negotiated separately) or tips. Additional time is charged in

RECOMMENDED MODES OF TRANSPORT

	Stazione Santa Lucia	Rialto	Ghetto
Stazione Santa Lucia	n/a	line 1 vaporetto 15min	walk 10min
Rialto	line 1 vaporetto 15min	n/a	walk 20min
Ghetto	walk 10min	walk 20min	n/a
Gallerie dell'Accademia	line 3 vaporetto 15min	walk 20min	line 82 vaporetto 20min
Piazza San Marco	line 3 vaporetto 25min	walk 15min	line 82 vaporetto 30min
Zanipolo	line 41/51 vaporetto 30min	walk 15min	line 42/52 vaporetto 20min

20-minute increments (day/night €40/50). You may be offered a price break in overcast weather or around midday, when other travellers get too hot and hungry for gondola rides. Agree in advance on a price, time limit and singing to avoid surcharges.

Gondolas cluster at *stazi* (stops) along the Grand Canal and near major monuments (including I Frari, Ponte dei Sospiri and Gallerie dell'Accademia), but you can also book one by phoning ☎ 041 5285075.

WATER TAXI
The James Bond way to get around town is on these sleek teak speedboats. Official rates start at €8.90, plus €1.80 per minute, €6 extra if the boat is called to your hotel, and more for night trips, luggage and large groups – so even short trips run from €60 to €90. But with unwieldy luggage or a group of 10 to 20, a water taxi may be the best way to reach your destination. Taxis are metered, but prices can also be negotiated in advance; a trip from Rialto to San Marco should cost around €60. You can book a water taxi by calling either ☎ 041 5222303 or ☎ 041 2406711.

Ignore water-taxi drivers at Piazzale Roma who claim there are no vaporetti stops nearby; the stops are in front of the bus terminal.

BUS
Buses run from Piazzale Roma (Map pp100–1, B4) to Mestre and other mainland destinations, as well as up and down the Lido. Tickets cost €1 (or €9 for 10 rides) at news-stands or tobacconists, and are good for an hour once validated in the machine on the bus. Schedules are posted at most stops and online at www.actv.it.

Gallerie dell'Accademia	Piazza San Marco	Zanipolo
line 2 vaporetto 20min	line 2 vaporetto 30min	line 41/51 vaporetto 30min
walk 20min	walk 15min	walk 15min
line 1 vaporetto 20min	line 1 vaporetto 35min	line 1 vaporetto 35min
n/a	walk 15min	walk 30min
walk 15min	n/a	walk 15min
walk 30min	walk 15min	n/a

PRACTICALITIES
BUSINESS HOURS
Hours during August and winter may vary, but businesses are usually open from 9am to 1pm and 3.30pm to 7.30pm Monday to Saturday. Restaurants and cafes are usually open Sunday and may be closed Monday or Tuesday. See inside front cover for more-specific opening hours.

DISCOUNTS
Chorus pass (☎ 041 2750462; www.chorus venezia.org; adult/EU student up to 29yr/family €10/7/20) offers single entry to16 Venetian churches and is valid for one year; it's for sale online and at participating churches.

The **Museum pass** (www.museicivici veneziani.it; adult/child €18/12) is valid for single entry to 11 museums over six months; a limited ticket offers entry to five Piazza San Marco museums for €13/7.50 per adult/

child. Passes are available online, at participating museums and the tourist office (p179).

See p175 for information on VeniceCard and Rolling Venice-Card.

HOLIDAYS
1 January	New Year's Day
6 January	Epiphany
March/April	Good Friday
March/April	Easter Monday
25 April	Liberation Day
1 May	Labour Day
15 August	Feast of the Assumption
1 November	All Saints' Day
8 December	Feast of the Immaculate Conception
25 December	Christmas Day
26 December	Boxing Day

INTERNET
To find out what's doing in Venice, check out these useful websites:
2venice (www.2venice.it) Lists select events, hotels, shops and nightlife.

A Guest in Venice (www.aguestinvenice.com) Hotelier association provides information on upcoming exhibitions, events and lectures.

Guardian Travel (www.guardian.co.uk /travel/venice) The UK paper and its readers offer tips on travel that's last minute, on the cheap, with dogs, and more.

My Local Guide (http://venezia.mylocalguide .org) Locals recommend personal favourite sights, restaurants and shops.

Venetian Club (www.thevenetianclub.co.uk) Local initiative to preserve Venetian culture offers hands-on courses, insider tours and discounts.

Venezia da Vivere (www.veneziadavivere .com) This is *the* guide to what's hip and happening in Venice now; it lists music performances, art openings, nightlife, new designers and more.

Venice Explorer (http://venicexplorer.net) Provides listings and locator maps for Venice's restaurants, shops and attractions.

Venice Tourist Board (www.turismovenezia .it) This site sells tickets to major city attractions; it also covers upcoming cultural events.

Weekend a Venezia (http://en.venezia.waf .it) Discounted and last-minute tickets to major tourist attractions.

The following are a selection of Venice's internet cafes:

Internet Point San Barnaba (Map pp110–11, D3; ☎ 041 2770926; Campo San Barnaba 2759, Dorsoduro; internet 20min €3; ☼ 9am-1.30pm & 3.30-7pm Mon-Sat)

Net Gate (Map pp110-11, D2; ☎ 041 2440213; Crosera San Pantalon, Dorsoduro; internet 1hr €8; ☼ 9.30am-7pm Mon-Sat)

VeNice (Map pp72-3, B5; ☎ 041 2758217; Rio Terà Lista di Spagna 149, Cannaregio; internet 1hr €8; ☼ 9am-11pm)

World House (Map pp60–1, B3; ☎ 041 52848 71; www.world-house.org; Calle della Chiesa 4502, Castello; internet 1hr/3hr €8/18; ☼ 10am-11pm)

LANGUAGE

A few choice words in Venetian will endear you to your hosts, especially at happy hour. To keep up with the *bacaro* (bar) banter, try mixing these phrases in with your Italian:

Cheers!	*Sanacapána!*
cheap wine	*brunbrún*
glass (of wine)	*ombra*
happy hour	*giro di ombra*
How lucky!	*Bénpo!*
It's all the same to me.	*De rufe o de rafe.*
Oh no!	*Siménteve!*
Perfect.	*In bróca.*
to become Venetian	*venexianárse*
to carouse	*far el samartinéto*
Watch out!	*Ócio!*
Welcome!	*Benvegnú!*
Yes sir!	*Siorsi!*
You bet!	*Figurárse!*
you guys	*voaltrí*
Venetian (m/f)	*venexiano/a*

MONEY

Italy uses the euro (€); see inside front cover for exchange rates.

Your accommodation will be your main expense in Venice, followed by meals, which start at €2 to €3 for a couple of *cicheti* (Venetian tapas) or a slice of pizza – although the sky's the limit at Harry's Bar. An *ombra* (glass) of wine or prosecco runs to €1.50 to €4, and espresso at the bar costs €0.80 to €1. Instead of buying bottled water, you can save money and the environment with a glass of mineral water at the bar for €0.20 to €0.50. When your feet get tired, hop on the vaporetto for €6.50. At €80 for 40 minutes, a gondola ride is not a means of transport – it's a main event, and a memorable way to explore the canals.

TELEPHONE

GSM and tri-band mobile phones can be used in Italy with a local SIM card; these can be purchased at Vodafone and Telecom Italia Mobile outlets across the city. Coin-operated orange Telecom Italia phone booths can be found around major piazzas.

COUNTRY & CITY CODES

When calling Venetian landlines, even from within the city, you must dial the ☎ 041 city code; local mobile numbers have no initial 0. To call from outside Italy, first dial the Italian country code (☎ 39).

USEFUL PHONE NUMBERS

See inside front cover for a list of useful phone numbers, including emergency numbers and directory assistance.

TIPPING

It is customary to leave a 10% tip at restaurants where service is not included in the bill, and you can leave small change at cafes. Hotel porters are tipped €1 per bag.

TOURIST INFORMATION

Venice has tourist offices run by **Azienda di Promozione Turistica** (APT; ☎ 041 5298711; www.turismovenezia.it) at a number of locations:

Marco Polo Airport (☽ 9.30am-7.30pm) In the arrivals hall.

Piazza San Marco (Map pp42-3, G5; Piazza San Marco 71f, San Marco; ☽ 9am-3.30pm Mon-Sat) Venice's main tourism office.

Piazzale Roma (Map pp100-1, B3; Santa Croce; ☽ 9.30am-1pm & 1.30-6.30pm Apr-Oct, until 4.30pm Nov-Mar)

Stazione Santa Lucia (Map pp72-3, B5; Cannaregio; ☽ 8am-6.30pm)

TRAVELLERS WITH DISABILITIES

A **disabled-assistance office** (Map pp72-3, B5; Stazione Santa Lucia, Cannaregio; ☽ 7am-9pm) is located in front of platform 4 at Stazione Santa Lucia. For further information on accessibility in Venice, try **Informahandicap** (Map pp42-3, G5; ☎ 041 2748144; www .comune.venezia.it/informahandicap; San Marco; ☽ 3-5pm Wed).

>INDEX

See also separate subindexes for See (p188), Shop (p189), Eat (p190), Drink (p191) and Play (p191).

000 map pages

000 map pages

🛍 SHOP

INDEX

000 map pages